UNITY AND DIVERSITY

CAC Publishing
Center for Action and Contemplation
cac.org

"*Oneing*" is an old English word that was used by Lady Julian of Norwich (1342–1416) to describe the encounter between God and the soul. The Center for Action and Contemplation proudly borrows the word to express the divine unity that stands behind all of the divisions, dichotomies, and dualisms in the world. We pray and publish with Jesus' words, "that all may be one" (John 17:21).

EDITOR:
Vanessa Guerin

ASSOCIATE EDITOR:
Shirin McArthur

PUBLISHER:
The Center for Action and Contemplation

ADVISORY BOARD:
David Benner
James Danaher
Ilia Delio, OSF
Sheryl Fullerton
Stephen Gaertner, OPraem
Ruth Patterson

Design and Composition by Nelson Kane

Cover: *Tree of Life*, engraving by David Klein, © 2018

© 2018 Center for Action and Contemplation.
All rights reserved.

Oneing
An Alternative Orthodoxy

The biannual literary journal of the Center for Action and Contemplation.

The Perennial Tradition, Vol. 1, No. 1, Spring 2013

Ripening, Vol. 1, No. 2, Fall 2013

Transgression, Vol. 2, No. 1, Spring 2014

Evidence, Vol. 2, No. 2, Fall 2014

Emancipation, Vol. 3, No. 1, Spring 2015

Innocence, Vol. 3, No. 2, Fall 2015

Perfection, Vol. 4, No. 1, Spring 2016

Evolutionary Thinking, Vol. 4, No. 2, Fall 2016

Transformation, Vol. 5, No. 1, Spring 2017

Politics and Religion, Vol. 5, No. 2, Fall 2017

Anger, Vol. 6, No. 1, Spring 2018

Unity and Diversity, Vol. 6, No. 2, Fall 2018

Oneing is a limited-edition publication; therefore, some editions are no longer in print. To order available editions of Oneing, please visit https://store.cac.org/.

Oneing

VOLUME 6 NO. 2

EDITOR'S NOTE

I'm encircled by a single thing, a single movement:
. . .
a distant empire of confused unities
reunites encircling me.

          —Pablo Neruda

I N HIS INTRODUCTION to this edition of *Oneing*, Richard Rohr writes: *"God has to be otherness—diversity, if you will—but God also has to be diversity overcome and resolved*—initially inside of the Deity Itself, then in all those who live inside of God, who are imprinted, marked, and 'turned into the image that they reflect.'" Rohr's description of God as a diversity is not unlike Neruda's understanding of the essence of unity.

The articles and poems in this edition of *Oneing* represent powerful expressions of diversity that weave together seamlessly into a superb collection. In her article, "Embracing Diversity through the Cosmic Principles," Franciscan Joan Brown offers an overview that sets the evolutionary stage for the edition. She writes, "What if we could realize that the very difference we cannot tolerate, or seem bent upon destroying, is actually responsible for our own well-being?"

Similarly, in "Unity and Diversity in the Land of Nonviolence," Catholic priest, pacifist, and proponent of nonviolence John Dear writes, "If we deny anyone their humanity, if we do not recognize everyone as a sister or a brother, if we oppose others who are different and seek to dominate everything according to our group or nation, we renounce God, reject Jesus, disregard the Gospel, and lose our vision. More fundamentally, we lose our humanity. We become inhuman."

LaVera Crawley describes a painful, visceral experience of inhumanity at the Grunewald Train Station, a former freight yard that served as one of three Berlin deportation points for Jews being sent to concentration camps. In her article, "The Vicarious Trauma of Hate," she describes "a solitude and an eeriness [she] couldn't quite name" at a memorial: "I soon noticed the inscriptions on the steel grates, each one marked chronologically by the day, month, and year of a particular transport, along with the number of Jews deported and the site of their final destination—names like Riga, Auschwitz, Sachsenhausen, and other ominous places…representing over fifty thousand Berlin Jews." The full impact of the inhumanity of the Holocaust, which traumatized and haunted her beyond her time in Germany, was exacerbated by the anti-immigrant rhetoric she encountered when she returned home to the US.

In her article, "My Challenging Journey from Diversity to Unity," Polly Baca, who suffered painful discrimination as a child because of the color of her skin, describes how she eventually transcended her experiences by understanding the struggles of other oppressed groups. Through her work with Martin Luther King, Jr., labor leaders and civil rights activists Cesar Chavez and Dolores Huerta, and presidential candidate Bobby Kennedy, she learned "that it was not only Mexican Americans that suffered from discrimination and hardship, but also other minorities, women, LGBTQ, the poor, disabled, and even some straight white men."

These cited authors give us a glimpse of what can happen if we pay attention and are fully present to one another, and the transformation we can experience by recognizing that diversity is not our enemy, but our teacher; not something to disdain, but to embrace. As Garridon Grady states in "Evolving in Diversity," "being confident that I'm a good person doesn't also mean that I don't have any work to do." Our work consists in being fully aware of and present to our brothers and sisters and all of creation that exists in unity "inside of God."

Each of the articles and poems in this edition of *Oneing* represents one complex facet of this underlying unity.

Vanessa Guerin,
Editor

CONTRIBUTORS

RICHARD ROHR, OFM, is a Franciscan priest of the New Mexico Province and the Founding Director of the Center for Action and Contemplation in Albuquerque, New Mexico. An internationally recognized author and spiritual leader, Fr. Richard teaches primarily on incarnational mysticism, non-dual consciousness, and contemplation, with a particular emphasis on how these affect the social justice issues of our time. Along with many recorded conferences, he is the author of numerous books, including *The Divine Dance: The Trinity and Your Transformation* (with Mike Morrell) and *Just This*. To learn more about Fr. Richard Rohr and the CAC, visit https://cac.org/richard-rohr/richard-rohr-ofm/.

JOAN BROWN, OSF, is a Franciscan sister of the Rochester, Minnesota community. Her Kansas farm roots, passion for the Sacred Earth Community, multicultural experiences in New Mexico, and many years of experience in the non-profit and social justice sectors inform her work as executive director of New Mexico Interfaith Power and Light. Sr. Joan participated in the 2009 United Nations Climate Change meeting in Copenhagen, Denmark and was an official observer with the Franciscans International NGO at the 2015 United Nations Climate Change Conference in Paris, France. In 2015, she was a White House Champions of Change recipient in the category of Climate Faith Leaders. She holds a master's degree from California Institute of Integral Studies. To learn more about Sr. Joan Brown, visit New Mexico Interfaith Power and Light, http://www.nm-ipl.org/staff-and-board/.

THE REV. JOHN DEAR is an internationally recognized voice and leader for peace and nonviolence. A priest, activist, author, and former Jesuit, he served as Director of the Fellowship of Reconciliation, the largest interfaith peace organization in the US. John has traveled the war zones of the world, led Nobel Peace-prize winners to Iraq, given thousands of lectures on peace across the US, and served as pastor of several churches in New Mexico. He recently helped draft Pope Francis' January 2017 World Day of Peace message on nonviolence. He is a co-founder of Campaign Nonviolence and the Nonviolent Cities Project and a Nobel Peace Prize nominee. His thirty-five books include *The Nonviolent Life, A Persistent Peace, The Questions of Jesus,* and *The God of Peace.* To learn more about John Dear, visit http://johndear.org/.

MICKY SCOTTBEY JONES is a healing justice practitioner, writer, speaker, and faith-rooted activist and organizer. The Director of Healing Justice with Faith Matters Network and a core team member with The People's Supper, she is a Justice Doula and mama-activist-contemplative-healer-holy-disrupter who believes in throwing parties as a key revolutionary strategy. She loves bringing people together to explore brave space, awaken empathy, and fight oppression. Recently named by *The HuffPost* as one of the Black Christian leaders changing the world, Micky encourages others to join her in moments of holy disruption and self-care in community. To learn more about Micky ScottBey Jones, visit http://www.mickyscottbeyjones.com/.

CARLOS NAVARRO is a journalist, blogger, and anti-hunger advocate. He currently works as a writer-editor for the University of New Mexico's Latin American and Iberian Institute. Carlos has been involved in faith-based anti-hunger advocacy for more than three decades, volunteering as a grassroots leader through the ecumenical organization Bread for the World. He also served on the board of directors of Bread for the World for twelve years. More recently, Carlos helped create the Interfaith Hunger Coalition, bringing people of faith in New Mexico to work together to end hunger in the state. To learn more about Carlos Navarro, visit https://laii.unm.edu/people/staff/carlos-navarro.html.

GIGI ROSS comes from Washington, DC, where she spent ten years working at the Shalem Institute for Spiritual Formation. Between leaving Shalem and joining CAC, she spent six years learning about trust while living in poverty and dependent on others for housing. Gigi provides administrative support for the Living School as CAC's Administrative Coordinator of Education. Gigi Ross may be contacted at giross@cac.org.

GIDEON TSANG is currently one of the pastors at Vox Veniae in East Austin, Texas, which pioneered Space 12, a unique non-profit collaborative space which serves as a neighborhood gathering point hosting art shows, concerts, slam poetry events, computer classes, dance classes, and a book exchange program for inmates, while partnering with neighborhood associations and varying organizations. Space 12 weaves links globally with partnerships in Afghanistan and India, and an anti-trafficking network. Space 12 was voted "Best New Collaborative Art and Volunteer Space" in the *Austin Chronicle*. To learn more about Gideon Tsang and Vox Veniae, visit https://voxveniae.com/.

POLLY BACA is a certified spiritual director, a graduate of the Denver Catholic Biblical School, and a facilitator of a weekly Centering Prayer course at the Federal Correctional Institution, Englewood, Colorado. She is currently on the volunteer staff of Contemplative Outreach of Colorado. Polly is the former President and CEO of the Latin American Research and Service Agency. She was the first woman of color elected to the Colorado State Senate and the first Latina in the United States to serve in both houses of her state legislature (1975–1986). In the 1990s, she served as Special Assistant to the President of the United States for Consumer Affairs. Polly is a former member of the Center for Action and Contemplation's Board of Directors and an alumna of the CAC's Living School for Action and Contemplation. To learn more about Polly Baca, visit https://en.wikipedia. org/wiki/Polly_Baca.

GARRIDON GRADY is the IT and Web Products Manager at the Center for Action and Contemplation, responsible for the technology interfaces and infrastructure that support the CAC's mission. He has a Bachelor of Science in Business Management, with a focus on Information Technology, and he is currently studying for his MBA. Garridon has contributed to the execution of the CAC's mission since April of 2017. His interests include creating artwork, organic soap making, and embracing the connection to the infinite nature of the moment. Garridon is a father of five, revels in the sincerity and authenticity of children, and values love above all else. Garridon Grady may be contacted at ggrady@cac.org.

SHIRIN MCARTHUR, MDIV, is a spiritual guide, writer, poet, and editor who lives in Arizona. She is a former CAC staff member and the Associate Editor of *Oneing*. Shirin leads online and in-person retreats and is a contemplative photographer. Shirin's award-winning blog is part of the Christian Century network. To read her blog and learn more about Shirin McArthur, visit https://shirinmcarthur.com/.

MICHELLE A. SCHEIDT is a Program Officer at the Fetzer Institute, whose mission is to help build the spiritual foundation for a loving world. Before joining Fetzer in 2011, Michelle lived and worked on the south side of Chicago for over twenty years. Her background includes program development and administration, nonprofit boards, group facilitation, pastoral ministry, hospital chaplaincy, and leading retreats. Michelle holds a Doctorate in Ministry from Chicago Theological Seminary; a Master of Arts in Pastoral Studies from Catholic Theological Union; and a Bachelor of Arts in English from Marian University, Indianapolis. She is bilingual in Spanish and English and has worked in multicultural settings in the US and Latin America. Michelle lives with her spouse, Barbara Crock, in the woods near Kalamazoo, Michigan.

DAVID M. COOK, MD, FAAFP, is Chief Innovation Officer and Senior Vice President of Community Engagement for Novant Health. David is a family physician who developed a large family medicine practice in Charlotte, North Carolina; created a community health clinic serving the uninsured and underinsured; developed one of the state's only non-academic affiliated family medicine residency programs designed to train physicians in holistic care; and serves as a board member of the Black AIDS Institute. His work includes healthcare transformation in support of The Quadruple Aim: advocating for universal healthcare and social determinants of health, advancing patient-centered physician-driven care, physician leadership development, and giving a voice to the excluded. Considered a change agent, David is an alumnus of the Center for Action and Contemplation's Living School. To learn more about David Cook and Novant Health, visit https://www.novanthealth.org.

LAVERA CRAWLEY, MD, MPH, is Chair of the Board of Directors for CAC and an alumna of the Living School's inaugural class. A physician, bioethicist, and certified chaplain educator known for her work on race-based health disparities for palliative and end-of-life care, she was formerly a Soros Faculty Scholar for the Project on Death in America and ethics advisor to the Centers for Disease Control and Prevention. In 2011, after an academic career of more than sixteen years at Stanford University, LaVera embarked on a new vocation in the art of spiritual companionship as a hospital chaplain, bringing together her work in medicine, ethics, social justice, teaching, research, and public health with her longstanding interest in spirituality. To learn more about LaVera Crawley, visit https://cac.org/leadership-spotlight-interview-with-lavera-crawley-2018-05-31-alumni-newsletter/.

LEE STAMAN, MLIS, is the Systems Librarian at the Center for Action and Contemplation. Currently his work is focused on cataloging everything Richard Rohr has said and written. Lee has a passion for the role of information and technology in the modern world along with a deep interest in the history of religious thought. He has degrees in philosophy and theology and resides in Seattle, Washington with his wife and two children, to whom he reads the Patristics to put them to sleep. Lee Staman may be contacted at lstaman@cac.org.

INTRODUCTION

G OD'S MAJOR PROBLEM in liberating humanity has become
apparent to me as I consider the undying recurrence of *hatred
of the other*, century after century, in culture after culture and
religion after religion.

The dualistic mind, upon which most of us were taught to rely, is
simply incapable of the task of creating unity. It automatically divides
reality into binary opposites and does almost all its thinking inside of
this highly limiting frame. It dares to call this choosing of sides "thinking" because that is all it knows how to do! "Really good" thinking
then becomes devising a strong argument for our side and against
another side, race, group, political party, or religion.

Can you think of an era or nation or culture that did not oppose
otherness? I do not think there has ever been such a sustained group.
There have been enlightened individuals, thank God, but never
established groups—not even churches, synagogues, or mosques, I
am sorry to say. The Christian Eucharist was supposed to model and
positively teach equality, but we even turned the Holy Meal into an
exclusionary game, *a religiously sanctioned declaration and division* into
groups of the worthy and the unworthy—as if *we* were worthy?

It seems we must have our *other*! It appears we do not know who
we are except by opposition and exclusion. Eucharist was supposed
to tell us who we are in a positive and inclusionary way, but we
are not yet well-practiced at this. We honestly do not know how to
do unity. Many cardinals and bishops are seriously fighting Pope
Francis because he thinks people in a second marriage can go to
communion. They made the Holy Meal into a "prize for the perfect"
and a "reward for good behavior" instead of medicine for our universal
sickness—which we all need. Now I see what our real sickness is.
Most Christians still do not know how to receive a positive identity
from God. Instead, they receive only a negative one foisted on them
by culture.

In recent months, I have read about the long history of anti-
Semitism in Christian Europe—at the highest levels of church and

culture, in almost every single European country. Even canonized saints thought Jews were the problem. Anti-Semitism only lessened in the centuries when we could fight Muslims on Crusades instead. "Where can my negative energy go?" is the only enduring question. It must be exported somewhere.

It never seems to occur to us that *we* are the negative energy, which then sees and also creates that negative energy in others. The ego refuses to see this in itself. Seeing takes foundational conversion from the egoic self and most have not undergone that transformation—including most clergy, who historically appear to be careerists more than searchers for God, love, or truth. If this is "how it is with the greenwood, what will it be with the dry" (see Luke 23:31)? We can only give away what we ourselves have experienced and become.

When there was no obvious other around, such as "sinners," Jews, or Muslims, we divided Christianity itself into warring groups of "heretics," which allowed us to waste five hundred years enlarging the mistrust, fear, and judgments between Catholics, the many Protestant churches, and distant Orthodox and Oriental churches—and, of course, they did the same with all of us.

Like many of you, I watched the extended PBS series on the Vietnam War. There we saw the totally blinding power of ideology, fear, and hatred, cultivated over many decades, justifying the killing of millions of people whose only real problem was that they were *other*. Yes, we created our excuses and explanations on both sides: communists, gooks, colonialists, French, Americans—even dividing the one ancient Vietnamese culture into North and South so they could kill one another. Then it took us fifty years to look back at it all with some degree of objectivity and see that it was all a charade, a hall of mirrors, a web of lies—and always about *the other*, who had to be righteously feared and destroyed. Both Democrats and Republicans lied to us then, yet our convenient binary system lasted—and continues to this day, with disastrous results for the health of our country.

Today we see unabashed racism, classism, and sexism return to America at the highest levels of our government. White privilege is back in charge and the outcry is faint. How naïve we were to think this was all behind us after the civil rights education we had in the 1960s. It seems every generation must be newly converted—and sincere conversion cannot be mandated by law. (This does not mean we should not try. Otherwise, the other has no protection from the unconverted.)

You who might have read my book on the Trinity, *The Divine Dance*, know where I am heading here. I believe this problem is so foundational to all of reality that it had to be overcome in the very nature of God—from the very beginning—and in all things created in the image of God, which is exactly *all things. God has to be otherness —diversity, if you will —but God also has to be diversity overcome and resolved* —initially inside of the Deity Itself, then in all those who live inside of God, who are imprinted, marked, and "turned into the image that they reflect" (see 2 Corinthians 3:18).

Allow me to summarize my point with the classic placeholder names for distinction, pluriformity, and otherness in the Christian definition of God: Father, Son, and Holy Spirit. You can use other words if you want, but make sure they are distinct and different—and lovingly relational words. The three must be maintained as three and understood as different from one another. Yet the infinite trust and flow between them is so constant, so reliable, so true, and so faithful that they are also completely one. They must be diverse, and they must be one—at the same time. The glue that preserves both truths is Infinite Love.

Our basic human problem has been resolved in the very nature of God, but unless we allow ourselves inside of that Infinite Flow, we ourselves will always remain the *three* but never the *one*. If we remain mere monotheists, we will try to impose a false uniformity but never know how to love, honor, and respect diversity. Most racists, nationalists, and classists I know are zealous monotheists, but never Trinitarian.

Like God, we must be both three and one: Diversity affirmed, protected, and overcome by One Shared Love.

Richard Rohr

Embracing Diversity through the Cosmic Principles

By Joan Brown

S EVERAL YEARS AGO, I was shopping with my sister Carol, who was born with Down Syndrome. Carol turned to me, very upset. "Why are those people staring at me?" she asked. "They are looking at you because you are so beautiful," I said. My sister then broke into a loving smile.

Carol has forty-three chromosomes. All people with Down Syndrome are born with one extra chromosome. While some might look upon this as a defect, I experience my sister's being different as a gift. Perhaps that extra chromosome should be called the beauty or radiance chromosome, for it creates her joyful, loving, and welcoming personality.

Sometimes, that which might be different or disturbing is actually a call to look more deeply into the soul-level meaning of our lives. This summer, I have looked at many disturbing scenes of fires, drought, flooding, and suffering, impacting both creatures and people. Their faces reflect the consequences of climate change, which is staring us right in the face.

Diversity plays a major part in what we must learn as we live with ecological degradation and the impact of the Anthropocene Age. Most of us are aware that we are losing the diversity of plant, animal, and insect species, and human cultures, at an alarming rate. In fact, we are living into the greatest extinction of species and diversity in 65 million years. One thing of which we may not be aware is the integral place that diversity holds in the very existence of life.

As I walk through life, crying tears for that which we are losing, and wondering how we have wandered so far from the path of recognizing all as sacred and part of ourselves, I am drawn again and again to the cosmic principles of existence. Passionist priest and eco-theologian Thomas Berry (1914–2009) and evolutionary cosmologist Brian Swimme wrote about these principles in their book, *The Universe Story*. Their work builds upon the cosmological investigations of paleontologist and Jesuit priest Pierre Teilhard de Chardin (1881–1955), which were also explored by the writer and mystic Beatrice Bruteau (1930–2014).

All of us who live, breathe, and walk upon this amazing, holy Mother Earth are called to understand the cosmic principles inherent in the interdependent energy dynamic that throbs through every element of life. Nothing exists without these three interdependent energies that emerged from the first flaring forth over 13.8 billion years ago: *differentiation* or *diversity; subjectivity, interiority,* or *essence;* and *communion* or *community* and *interconnectedness.* These energies offer vital lessons for the critical and conflictual times in which we live, where diversity causes conflict, living is often at a superficial level, and individualism runs rampant.

DIVERSITY

FIRST, EVERY ONE of us—every human being, every drop of water, every molecule, every bird, each grain of sand, and each mountain—is *distinct* or *different*. Each is a unique manifestation

"We are here to awaken from the illusion of our separateness."

of Divine Love Energy. The universe thrives upon, and cannot exist without, diversity. The very differences that we shun, avoid, or even destroy are necessary for life to continue in a multitude of magnificent forms. This does not mean it is easy to embrace or even understand diversity, but it is a precious necessity. Diversity is responsible for creating our amazing and complex planet.

We might ask ourselves why we hate people or creatures that are different than ourselves. What if we could realize that the very difference we cannot tolerate, or seem bent upon destroying, is actually responsible for our own well-being?

When I travel back to my home farm in Kansas each summer, I always delight to see the wild iris, milkweed, and grasses growing in ditches alongside the fields. I know their presence speaks of wise farmers and county road services who do not mow such diversity down to the quick. Plant diversity creates a home for bees, monarch butterflies, finches, nesting rabbits, and quail. Cutting down these plants destroys homes and beauty, just as our tendency to create monoculture neighborhoods, schools, or community groups does not allow for the creative pollination of ideas and rich harvest of projects that might help us move into a sacred and viable future.

ESSENCE

THE SECOND COSMIC PRINCIPLE, *interiority* or *essence*, is more easily understood by people of all religious traditions. Every created thing is holy. Every blade of grass, grasshopper, child, and element is holy. Ecological degradation, racism, discrimination, hate, and disinterest in working for justice and love each speak to the lack of honoring the interiority of that which stands before me. Thomas Berry said that we no longer hear the voice of the rivers or mountains. I would add that we no longer hear the voice of our suffering brothers and sisters because everything and many people have become "it." Our lack of sense of presence in the other has eliminated knowing the "thou," or inner spirit, within all that exists.

As our ability to see with eyes of reverence and wonder deteriorates, so does our ability to embrace and understand differences. The path of greater human and ecological degradation is strewn with examples: people of color disproportionately filling our prisons, families from other cultures that we do not allow across our borders, young people whom we incarcerate, oceans filled with plastic islands, and natural islands submerged by rising oceans.

I am in love with seeds. I marvel at how different bean seeds, which look identical, create unique plants. I am amazed that each apricot tree has its own unique story, creating one-of-a-kind progeny. What mystery! That deep place within each thing, and everyone that holds the kernel of identity and spirit, whispers of the Holy and births diversity.

Thomas Berry, in his book *The Great Work*, profoundly addresses the degradation of humans and the natural world at the expense of the sacred within: "Physical degradation of the natural world is also the degradation of the interior world of the human."[1]

My work with New Mexico Interfaith Power and Light addresses climate change and climate justice. I work with diverse religious traditions. But the work to curb and address climate change is more than an "issue." In order to help people adjust and cope with climate change, which is the most critical concern of our day, I believe we must get in touch with the sacred essence of everything that exists. Our indigenous brothers and sisters have much to teach us about the sacred essence. Saints Francis and Clare of Assisi offer us models of how to live with all of creation as brother and sister, sharing the sacred and unique path with bird, herb, and brother wolf alike.

The universe thrives upon, and cannot exist without, diversity.

COMMUNITY

THE THIRD COSMIC PRINCIPLE, *communion* or *community*, is intimately linked to differentiation/diversity and interiority/ essence. A quote attributed to Thich Nhat Hanh states it well: "We are here to awaken from the illusion of our separateness." The gravitational pull of love draws everyone and everything into relationship and communion. All the great world religions have teachings about the greatest commandments being love of God or Dharma or the Holy One or Creator, and then love of neighbor as self. While we now comprehend that "neighbor" includes every atom, cow, drop of water, or tomato plant, we have yet to understand this deeper meaning.

Perhaps, as Beatrice Bruteau wrote, *"If we cannot love our neighbor as ourself, it is because we do not perceive our neighbor as ourself."*[2] If we are unable to see that we are in communion with another, we will not realize that what we do to ourselves, we do to the other and to the earth. Likewise, we do not realize that, ultimately, our lack of understanding turns back toward us in violence, whether that is fear of other races and diversity or destruction of Earth because we see the natural world as an object rather than a subject with interiority.

Each unique society in the world can be seen anew by understanding the cosmic principles. Even our activism and the issues we address can be viewed in light of science and the cosmic principles, thus offering new understandings and ways to act for the sake of the future.

We are moving into a very challenging and exciting time. No longer can we work with blinders on or in isolated silos, trying to address pet projects or particular issues of concern. This is one of the valuable lessons from the Rev. William Barber, one of the co-leaders of the Poor People's Campaign and founder of the Moral Monday movement. He sought to bring together people of diverse backgrounds, classes, and races in a moral movement, holding together overarching issues of racism, poverty, militarism, and ecological degradation. Not everyone worked on all these concerns, but everyone held a consciousness of the diverse concerns and worked in communion for the common good because everything intersects.

Pope Francis offers us another example of the communion of diverse concerns in the fourth chapter of *Laudato Sí*, when he explores the worldview of integral ecology.

Since everything is closely interrelated, and today's problems call for a vision capable of taking into account every aspect of the global crisis, I suggest that we now consider some elements of an *integral ecology*, one which clearly respects its human and social dimensions.[3]

Laudato Sí goes on to explain that ecology is the study of relationships and the environments in which they develop. Applied to human societies within the natural world, it is an integral ecology. Nothing is independent and "the fragmentation of knowledge and the isolation of bits of information can actually become a form of ignorance, unless they are integrated into a broader vision of reality."[4]

We are called to be larger than who we can imagine being in this moment. The cosmic principles are a new way of understanding, seeing, and acting in a world that seems to be torn apart by a misunderstanding of the beauty of diversity, the holiness of essence, and the evolutionary pull of communion.

As we face uncertain and troubling times, Thomas Berry offers an interesting insight.

The greatest of human discoveries in the future will be the discovery of human intimacy with all those other modes of being that live with us on this planet, inspire our art and literature, reveal that numinous world whence all things come into being, and with which we exchange the very substance of life.[5]

Our hearts break open often these days and weeks. Many of us sense that we are only beginning to enter an era when we face unfathomable destruction of life and beauty on a daily basis. We have not learned the lesson my sister Carol offered me about the one who seems different. The one with an extra chromosome mirrors beauty, carries a sacred essence, and can draw us into the communion of love when we most need it.   •

Half-and-Half

You can't be, says a Palestinian Christian
on the first feast day after Ramadan.
So, half-and-half and half-and-half.
He sells glass. He knows about broken bits,
chips. If you love Jesus you can't love
anyone else. Says he.

At his stall of blue pitchers on the Via Dolorosa,
he's sweeping. The rubbed stones
feel holy. Dusting of powdered sugar
across faces of date-stuffed mamool.

This morning we lit the slim white candles
which bend over at the waist by noon.
For once the priests weren't fighting
in the church for the best spots to stand.
As a boy, my father listened to them fight.
This is partly why he prays in no language
but his own. Why I press my lips
to every exception.

A woman opens a window—here and here and here—
placing a vase of blue flowers
on an orange cloth. I follow her.
She is making a soup from what she had left
in the bowl, the shriveled garlic and bent bean.
She is leaving nothing out.

—Naomi Shihab Nye[1]

Unity and Diversity in the Land of Nonviolence

By John Dear

I BELIEVE IN THE ESSENTIAL unity of man and, for that matter, of all that lives," Mahatma Gandhi once wrote.[1] He thought all life was sacred, that we are all one, all sisters and brothers of one another, even one with all creatures and Mother Earth.

This foundational spiritual truth led Gandhi to the conviction that nonviolence was now a normative requirement for every human being if we are to honor our sacred unity. If every living human being is our very sister or brother, we would never dare hurt anyone, much less sit back silently or passively in the face of global suffering, endless wars, poverty, and killing. Neither can we ignore the millions of creatures going extinct because of our systemic violence or remain indifferent in the face of systemic greed and the potential for environmental destruction from nuclear weapons. Knowing our oneness with creation, we would never harm Mother Earth or passively sit back while others unearth fossil fuels, heedless of the consequences of climate change.

We are all one, and so we try to practice meticulous, creative nonviolence toward every one, every creature, and Mother Earth.

Through his long search into the truth of our common unity and its requisite requirement of steadfast nonviolence, Gandhi came to celebrate the diversity of life everywhere—among all humans, all sentient beings, and creation itself. He learned that this nonviolent openness to our common unity leads to the celebration of diversity in all its forms. These seemingly disparate sides of reality point us to our generous God—Creator, Christ, and Spirit—a loving God of unity and diversity.

❧

I WRITE THESE WORDS by hand on a hot summer evening on the mesa where I live in northern New Mexico, looking out over a hundred miles of sagebrush, junipers, arroyos, and distant mountains. The sun sets in the distance, setting off a wild explosion of red, orange, and yellow colors against the blue sky.

The daily news breaks the heart with reports of never-ending war, bombings, gun violence, racism, sexism, the mistreatment of immigrants and prisoners, nuclear threats, wildfires, drought, and catastrophic climate change. Each day brings new evidence of how we have lost sight of our common unity and beautiful diversity. This systemic blindness is killing us—spiritually, emotionally, and physically.

In the distance, I see the mountains of Los Alamos, where the first atomic bomb was built over seventy years ago, where tens of thousands of others have been built since, and where business is booming today, thanks in large part to the thousands of devout, rich, faithful, church-going Christians who work there.

Seeing both the glories of creation spread out before me and the potential for the end of the world in the distant nuclear labs, I ponder once again the lesson of Gandhi—that since we are all one, fashioned by a loving Creator to live in peace and love with one another in this earthly paradise, we are invited to pursue the ancient wisdom of nonviolence: put down our swords, dismantle our weapons, vow never to harm anyone, return to our right minds, and receive the gift of vision. That pursuit led Gandhi to set off on a journey to universal love, universal compassion, and universal peace. He thought that was the path set out before every human being. Along the way, we discover and recognize new depths of our common unity and celebrate new layers of our glorious diversity.

-●

EARLIER THIS YEAR, I crisscrossed the country on a three-month, fifty-city speaking tour about my new book, *They Will Inherit the Earth: Peace and Nonviolence in a Time of Climate Change*. My thesis is that Jesus' third beatitude offers a beautiful way forward in this insane culture of violence, war, and environmental destruction. Thomas Merton wrote that "meekness" was the biblical word for active, Gandhian nonviolence, so I translate Jesus' teaching as, "Blessed are people of active, creative nonviolence; they will be one with creation, all humanity, all creatures, and Mother Earth."

In the course of writing the book, I spent time with friends at Tewa Women United in the Santa Clara Pueblo, the second poorest county in the nation. Seventy-five years ago, the US military barreled through, stole half their land—including the Los Alamos mountain, and built their nuclear-weapons laboratories there. From the start, they literally dumped the radioactive waste off the cliffs, down onto the indigenous people of the pueblo, poisoning the land, spreading cancer, and ensuring their permanent poverty.

As I write in the book, I asked one of the elders, my friend Marian Naranjo, about her long journey and Jesus' third beatitude. She shared

Along the way, we discover and recognize new depths of our common unity and celebrate new layers of our glorious diversity.

about the indigenous way of peace and nonviolence. She said that her people have been living that beatitude for centuries. They live and breathe at one with all humanity, all creatures, and Mother Earth, in their day-to-day peaceableness. They not only celebrate diversity, but learn from the diversity around them: in each other; in the creatures; in water, land, plants, trees, and sky; so they can better live at peace with each other. As they learn from the diversity in nature and honor each other's gifts, they also learn more about the Creator. In other words, unity and diversity, within the framework and geography of nonviolence, helps deepen their culture of peace and devotion to the God of peace, the Creator.

THE MYSTERY and scandal of Christianity is that God is nonviolent. It's right there in the Sermon on the Mount, from which Gandhi read every day for over forty years: "Blessed are the peacemakers; they shall be called the sons and daughters of God.... I say to you, love your enemies and pray for those who persecute you, that you may be sons and daughters of your heavenly God; for God makes the sun rise on the bad and the good and causes the rain to fall on the just and the unjust" (see Matthew 5:9, 44–45).

There, in the most radical, hard-hitting, political, revolutionary sentence in the entire Bible, in this call for universal, nonviolent love for those targeted with death by any nation/state, the nonviolent Jesus clearly describes the nature of God. God practices universal, nonviolent love.

Jesus teaches that God is nonviolent and that to be human is to be nonviolent. We are all called to be nonviolent. To deepen our awareness of our common human unity and glorious diversity, we have to deepen into total, universal nonviolence, into the very nature of God. That is the spiritual journey that lies ahead of every human being.

But, in fact, we not only ignore and deny our unity and diversity; we wage permanent war against unity and diversity—literally. War kills our sisters and brothers. In our willingness to support warfare, we declare, "We are not one." We label others as non-human, as enemies, as disposable, as objects suitable for death. Along the way, we join the business of death and serve the idols of death.

To reject the culture of disunity and destruction, to embrace human unity and celebrate diversity, is to practice nonviolence.

If we deny anyone their humanity, if we do not recognize everyone as a sister or a brother, if we oppose others who are different and seek to dominate everything according to our group or nation, we renounce God, reject Jesus, disregard the Gospel, and lose our vision. More fundamentally, we lose our humanity. We become inhuman.

To honor and celebrate human unity and diversity means living within the boundaries of nonviolence. There, we refuse to hurt or kill another person. We non-cooperate with the culture of violence, war, and killing. We do our best to stop the violence and killings. We do our part to build up the global grassroots movements of nonviolence to transform our world into a new culture of peace and nonviolence.

As people of contemplative nonviolence, we pursue our sacred unity and diversity with all 7.6 billion human beings, and all creatures, and Mother Earth too. We practice active nonviolence, prophetic nonviolence, and visionary nonviolence, as Jesus taught in the Sermon on the Mount. We seek first God's reign here on earth—which Gandhi defined as nonviolence everywhere on earth—as the spiritual landscape of nonviolence. Awareness of unity and diversity summons us not only to a whole new attitude toward life, but also to public action for justice, disarmament, creation, and peace.

❧

J ESUS LIVED, TAUGHT, and practiced active, creative nonviolence. Even his last words to his followers in his little community were a plea for nonviolence: "Put down the sword" (see Matthew 26:52). In the end, I think he calls us to live *eschatological nonviolence*, to act as if we are already in the reign of God's total, universal nonviolence. In this landscape, we live in sacred unity every day, every moment, with every word, with every breath.

At the river Jordan, Jesus learns that he is the beloved of God and realizes that everyone is the beloved of God. He goes forth to call everyone to claim our true identities as beloved sons and daughters of God—as peacemakers, as sisters and brothers of one another, as people of universal, nonviolent love. But he knows well how unaware and blind we are, and how determined we are to crush, dominate, and

To reject the culture of disunity and destruction, to embrace human unity and celebrate diversity, is to practice nonviolence.

destroy that unity and diversity. That's when he sets off to Jerusalem on a campaign of nonviolence, to confront systemic destruction head-on. At one point, after he reveals his True Self in the transfiguration, he teaches his disciples to leave their spiritual comfort zone on the mountaintop and follow him down the mountain, into the public fray of the grassroots movement for justice. This is the journey of those who honor sacred unity and diversity.

When he finally arrives in Jerusalem, he breaks down weeping over our failure to understand our sacred unity and diversity ("If only you had understood the things that make for peace," he laments in Luke 19:42). He then goes into the Temple, where he turns over the tables of injustice where the religious authorities cooperate with the empire to make money off the poor. "No more injustice," he proclaims. He undertakes symbolic, nonviolent, civil disobedience. He's not mad or angry; he's grieving. (I understand this from experience—having been arrested some eighty times, I've learned that anger and yelling only provoke the authorities and violate our meticulous Gospel of nonviolence.) Jesus' nonviolent pursuit of unity, like Gandhi's and Martin Luther King, Jr.'s, leads to nonviolent public action and its consequences.

So, what is the lesson? The Gospel portrays the fulfillment of the contemplative realization of our common sacred unity with one another and all creation as the difficult public journey into the fray, to speak out and take action in grassroots movements of nonviolence to stop the killings and the destruction of creation. It entails the willingness to help build global, grassroots, nonviolent movements for justice and disarmament. This unpleasant, untidy, unfulfilling, often frustrating, nearly hopeless, unsuccessful, ineffective work is the fullness of the spiritual life. It's the journey of the cross in the footsteps of the nonviolent Jesus, from Galilee to our own Jerusalems, to confront our own empire and call for a new culture of peace, nonviolence, and global unity, with all its social, economic, and political implications.

With this in mind, my Pace e Bene friends and I organized the fifth national week of action, September 15–23, 2018. CampaignNonvio-lence.org sponsored over two thousand marches and events against war, poverty, racism, and environmental destruction, and in support of a new culture of peace and nonviolence. This grassroots organizing is our way of upholding our unity and diversity. Around the world, billions of people are engaged in the power of grassroots movements supporting nonviolence. The recent Parkland students' March for our Lives shows how this methodology of active nonviolence can awaken new, widespread awareness of our common unity.

We all do our part to continue Jesus' campaign of nonviolence. Together, as movement people of eschatological nonviolence, we are entering a new land of nonviolence and heralding that day when there are no more wars, no more racism, no more sexism, no more poverty, no more starvation, no more gun violence, no more torture, no more executions, no more nuclear weapons, and no more environmental destruction.

We go forward in this beautiful campaign of peace, come what may, because we know that, in our beautiful diversity, surrounded by the glories of creation, with the eyes of faith and hope, with sacred hearts of universal love, in the spirit of resurrection peace, in the land of nonviolence, we are already one. •

For You and for Me

I'm stepping more towards love.
I'm stepping more towards freedom.
I'm stepping more towards honesty.
I'm stepping more towards dignity.

For you. For me.

I'm taking greater risk for peace.
I'm taking greater risk for justice.
I'm taking greater risk for what is ours, not what is mine.
I'm taking greater risk for mother nature.

For you. For me.

I'm making more room to sit with you…in pain, in longing,
    in loss.
I'm making more room to sit with myself…in pain, in longing,
    in loss.
I'm making more room to invite you to sit with me…in
    pain, in longing, in loss.

For you. For me.

I'm going to hug you harder.
I'm going to hug you longer.
I'm going to let you…hug me.

For you. For me.

I'm buying less.
I'm giving more.
I'm wasting less.
I'm planting more.

For you. For me.

I'm spending more time with trees.
I'm spending more time with children.
I'm spending more time with elders.
I'm spending more time in silence.

For you. For me.

I'm reaching across the aisle.
I'm reaching across the street.
I'm reaching across the divide.
I'm reaching…further into me.

For you. For me.

More love.
More freedom.
More healing.
More rest.
More time.
More spirit.
More vulnerability.
More nature.
More wisdom.
More humility.

For you. For me.

—Jonathon Stalls[1]

The Narratives that Make Us

By Micky ScottBey Jones

WHO ARE YOUR people?
You have "people," even if you don't know your DNA, even if your family tree is full of broken branches and root rot. You have people even if you reject the choices of your ancestors and can only piece together parts of your past. Like a character in a play, you have a backstory and, just like the actor playing the role, you have a responsibility to add depth and understanding to that backstory. Why? Because, just like in a play, a character with no roots, no depth, no sense of what they carry into each scene is unable to connect to others and to the wider unfolding narrative of the human drama. True connection, which is the foundation of a beloved community, happens when you understand your own story and how it connects to the stories of others and the metanarrative of the human struggle.

I carry many peoples in my bones and all through my body, my spirit, and my history. In my DNA, I am the legacy of those, as James

H. Cone writes, who "are made brother and sister by the blood of the lynching tree, the blood of sexual union, and the blood of the cross of Jesus."[1] In my flesh, I carry the terrifying, messy, and yet, sometimes still-beautiful, parallel and intersecting stories of the people who, by force and by choice, have come to live in Turtle Island (North America).

Responsible, nuanced, and complex knowledge of the stories I carry in my body did not come installed at my birth like a computer's operating system—at least not in a conscious way that I could observe and critique, and with which I could wrestle. Challenges and encounters in my life provided the opportunities along the way for the work of "identity development," as described in *The Power of Stories*, by the Rev. Jacqueline J. Lewis. The work of sorting through the stories that make up the "living text," or story of self, that we each carry, is a lifelong task of taking the stories we are given by society, family, and media, and that originate in the self, and, as Lewis writes, "finding one's narrative voice in conversation with multiple, overlapping and (sometimes) conflicting stories."[2] It is a conscious process—no one arrives at a clear understanding of their identity by accident. For those who wish to engage in the work of bringing more love, justice, and *shalom* into the world, we must start with the particularities of the stories that converge with our own story of identity or risk colliding with the stories of others in damaging ways.

WE ARE IN a time of great social transformation. We are in a time where the past is covered by a rosy haze that makes it seem simpler, purer, and less confusing, while the present is covered in literal and figurative tear gas that obscures the current story in ways we may only see when the gas clears. In many respects, we are in a time of rapid innovation, witnessing achievements that are a fulfillment of our ancestors' wildest dreams, and social change largely consisting of a more inclusive, open, connected world. At the same time, we are in great physical and ideological danger as white supremacy evolves, manipulates, and claws its way to control. Additionally, we humans are still learning to adapt to this digital age, where we must learn to survive an "age of loneliness"—magnified by hyper-connectivity, hyperbolic storytelling, and social media climbs and crashes—that leaves each of us vulnerable to feeling alone, isolated, ignored, or forgotten.

I believe, against much of the evidence of human history, that the moral arc of the universe is slightly tilted toward justice. I believe it is our responsibility to participate in the social transformation of our time by reaching up, with the stories of our individual lives, to further bend the moral arc of the universe toward justice. I believe in the wisdom of creation that reminds us that life persists, not despite, but because of, death. Each human narrative contains weight that can help bend the universe toward justice, but does not automatically do so. The questions that align with these responsibilities are: "Will you use your life, your narrative, to add justice to the overall human story?" "Will you birth life into the world, working with whatever material, living and dead, to which you have access?"

This social transformation is woven together by narratives that help us understand our larger cultural contexts. My own narrative—who I am, who I come from, and the people, places, and experiences that have made me who I am—forms the lens through which I process the narratives of the wider culture and society, not the other way around. These overarching narratives are often supremacist, imperialist, oppressive, and simplified. These metanarratives—good and bad, light and dark, heroic and villainous—cast a long shadow on the narratives of personal and social change and complicate them. Individuals who do not believe they have a personal narrative—who are unaware of their own ancestral history, place, and character traits—are unable to productively interact with metanarratives. Those who cannot wrestle with the contradictions and complexities of their own narratives will have and cause problems as well. There is a cognitive dissonance caused by holding on to the oppressive narratives given to us by the larger stories of Western cultural imperialists. The responsibility of liberation, then, is to learn to read our own and others' complex stories, so as to edit and retell them.

The parallel and divergent narratives of others show me that my narrative is one of many in the tapestry of humanity. There are narratives of domination, supremacy, and fear that seduce people into believing the myth of violence is the most powerful and legitimate form of redemption. Despite the human proclivity to believe only in a single story, we can hold multiple narratives at the same time, weaving what we think we know into a larger tapestry.

Our stories matter, not just because we come to know who we are, but because knowing them allows us to walk in the power and truth

What narratives
are calling you to cultivate
your strong roots to engage
at intersections of difference?

they contain. Our stories are the compass of our personal and social transformation in the world.

In order to work in deep, meaningful, impactful solidarity with others, I must actually become more deeply rooted in my own story. It is in knowing who I am that I am able to understand *how* to relate to those with whom I wish to organize and build.

Our human brains naturally want to find similarities. I need, for example, to find what my friend Andrea, a Jew, and I, a Christian, have in common, so that I can make sense of our relationship. However, I believe it is harder, richer, more rooted work to recognize that our faiths and our beliefs may have significant differences and particularities that we do not share, and for which we learn to make space. It is intellectually, spiritually, and relationally lazy to only focus on our similarities as core to how we care for one another and organize together. I do not want you to care about me because I could be your sister. I want you to care about me, not because I am like anyone with whom you are related or for whom you care, but because I am a human being, worthy of love, belonging, and freedom.

As part of a collaborative project called The People's Supper, I am part of a group that encourages and trains people to host others, using the practices of personal storytelling over shared meals for healing and bridging conversations. Since the 2016 election, we've been the catalyst that has brought more than four thousand people together to share their food and stories. We craft questions that invite sharing stories of belonging and longing, of disappointment and hope, and of personal and social transformation. Telling our stories helps us engage each other with more clarity. Listening to the stories of others reminds us that we are similar and *different* from others—all of us deserving of liberation and love.

Sustainable leadership is narrative-rooted leadership. If you want to be involved in the current struggle for liberation for all of creation for your lifetime—and I hope you do, because we need each and every one of us, with the weight of our stories—you need to be deeply rooted in your story, which is rooted in relationship, which is rooted in people.

What narratives are calling you to cultivate your strong roots to engage at intersections of difference?

One of the ways I have cultivated the roots of my particular narrative is to learn more about the ScottBeys. My surname on my father's side is ScottBey. When my great-grandparents became members of the Moorish Science Temple—a uniquely American expression of nationality and religion—they added Bey to the Scott and became ScottBey. My people, those ancestors who added the Bey to Scott, lived in the 1920s, a time of great social transformation. They knew they had to have their own story about who they were and who their people were. My 91-year-old grandfather, Earl ScottBey, Sr., who was raised in the temple but has since become a deacon in the Baptist church, says of our family, "We have always been people of faith." From stories he has gifted me, I know they were a people that were determined to express their faith in a way that was different and set apart in appearance, word, and action. They would have no part in war; developed pro-Black, multi-dimensional education; and lived in deep, interdependent community, taking care of the practical, educational, and spiritual needs of one another, including my great-grandmother, who was the community midwife.

They answered the question, "Who are your people?" by rejecting how others defined them—white, Black, or otherwise—reclaiming identity as people that had their own land, their own religion, and a way of life that included a deep commitment to care for one another and contribute to the larger society in helpful, life-giving ways. They were a people with a larger story, with an origin in freedom, faithfulness, and self-determination.

Their narrative is part of my narrative. I continue the narrative of those who traveled north as a part of the great migration, of those who educated their children on the history, wisdom, and beliefs of their people—even if it was after school and on weekends—and of those who rename, redefine, and reconnect in order to live flourishing lives in the midst of oppression and rampant white supremacy.

I also come from the narrative of people who struggled to maintain community and navigate destructive internal conflict. I see warnings and wisdom in their chapters of the narrative. Their chapters don't define me; instead, they give me context, historical placement, recognition of themes, and the wisdom of those who have been in similar situations. I know my particularity brings me closer to some stories and pushes me further from others.

In addition to my own experience, I come from particular narratives of Blackness, of American enslaved people Blackness, and of religious innovation, social activism, and diversity. My task is to ask myself questions like, "What privileges do I carry because of my ancestors?" and "What are the historic and current struggles of people who look like me, who carry the name Bey or EL?" and "What are my responsibilities to the generations behind me and before me?" I don't come into this human story with the same narrative as those whose European ancestors came through Ellis Island or owned land and people. I share some overlapping narrative with other Black and People of Color while realizing that our stories flow into and out of intersecting and parallel streams. My life, my work, my relationships, and my spirituality are more grounded when I am grounded in my own story that becomes even more liberated as I stand in solidarity with those in any struggle against injustice.

Nikki Giovanni said, "If you don't understand yourself, you don't understand anybody else."[3] The more I understand my roots and my particularities, the more honestly and clearly I engage others. We do not have to share the same struggles for me to understand that your liberation is tied up with mine. As I understand myself, my people, and my roots, I more fully understand where my individual privilege, power, and places of marginalization connect to others *and* my responsibilities in the struggle against the systems of domination that impact entire communities in particular ways.

Who are your people? What is your story? How will you engage these living texts in order to responsibly, lovingly, and creatively engage the narrative of beloved community?

Finding Collaborative Unity on the Issue of Hunger

By Carlos Navarro

T HE CALLING TO FEED the hungry is both individual and collective. For those like me, who are called to take action against hunger and to care for the needs of our neighbors, our ministry is very clear. "God wants us to feed the hungry," says the Rev. Larry Bernard,[1] a Franciscan priest who serves Jemez Pueblo and other communities in New Mexico.

My own calling first came as a high school student in the 1970s, when I read two articles, side by side, in the newspaper. One piece addressed the high levels of military spending on the part of the US government, while the other article discussed an increase in world hunger. What a no-brainer it would be, I thought, to divert some of the large sums of money being spent for defense purposes into reducing hunger! Then the divine gift of discernment kicked in. I felt called to make disparity the focus of my ministry, first through the ecumenical, faith-based, advocacy organization Bread for the World and later through the Interfaith Hunger Coalition (IHC) in New Mexico.

Individual commitment is not enough, however. Our own individual paths are less effective if they are not part of a larger collective action. To take action against hunger in our local communities, as well as in our nation and globally, we need people of faith and conscience who have a vision and vocation to work in a collaborative manner, whether this comes in the form of direct service, advocacy, education, or a combination of the three.

The mandate for individuals to come together as community to act to end hunger and care for those who lack basic necessities is found in our holy scriptures and in the words of important figures across faith traditions. In almost all religious traditions, the connection between our relationship with God and with our neighbor is at the core of our beliefs. This is especially evident during holy periods such as Lent, Yom Kippur, and Ramadan, when we fast not only to honor the Creator, but to feel the pain of those who lack the basic necessities of life. At the End Hunger Summit in Albuquerque, New Mexico in September 2017, several members of the IHC underscored this basic tenet of our beliefs during a collaborative keynote address.

"Our vision is based on and motivated by our faith. Feeding the hungry and helping the poor is an integral part of Islamic faith," said Rabia Sahin Orhan, a leader of the Raindrop Women's Association in New Mexico, which, along with the Dialogue Institute Southwest, is part of the IHC family in New Mexico. "The Muslim is called to feed the hungry and help those in need, regardless of race, religion, or background. It's such an important part of the religion."[2]

In describing her own conviction to work to end hunger, Sahin Orhan cited the words of the prophet Muhammad, who said, "A person is not really a Muslim if he goes to bed satiated while his neighbor goes hungry."[3]

The concept is similar in Judaism. Rabbi Allen Maller writes, "First of all, fasting teaches compassion. It is easy to talk about the world's problem of hunger. We can feel sorry that millions of people go to bed hungry each day. But not until one can actually feel it in one's own body is the impact truly there. Compassion based on empathy is much stronger and more consistent than compassion based on pity. This feeling must lead to action."[4]

"We are taught that God created the world, and every human being is created in God's image and is entitled to have his or her basic needs met. If one cannot meet those needs, then it is the community's responsibility to help out," said Rachel Sternheim, education director at Congregation Albert, in her portion of the End Hunger Summit collaborative keynote address.[5]

The Baha'i faith also has a strong fasting component, which takes place during a nineteen-day period each March. The primary purpose of the fast is to eliminate the distractions that keep us from becoming holy. As the Baha'i holy man Abdu'l-Bahá (1844–1921) taught, our hearts are purified when we fast from the appetites of the body, including eating and drinking. David Langness explains how our personal fasting brings us closer to our neighbors: "While you're fasting, think back on the entire year and ask yourself: What can I do in this coming year to make my life and the lives of others better? How can I be of service to humanity?"[6]

Gabriela Marques, a member of the Albuquerque Baha'i Community, points out that this period of discernment is closely related to the philosophy of caring for the poor and feeding the hungry. "The Baha'i faith is very deeply interested and committed in the struggle against hunger, the provision of food for every member of the human race," Marques said in her portion of the Summit collaborative address. "As Baha'i, we understand that it's not just a matter of production and distribution, but a spiritual problem,"[7] said Marques, who once served as an intern for the World Food Program's Center for Excellence against Hunger in Brazil.

THE DUAL CONCEPT of honoring our Creator and feeding the hungry was a central theme of a World Food Day Celebration in Albuquerque in October 2016, an event that the IHC co-hosted with New Mexico Interfaith Power and Light (NMIPL). One of the prayer leaders was Matthew Shoulders, a member of the Oglala Lakota of South Dakota who has lived at Isleta Pueblo for almost a dozen years. He offered a prayer for humanity in his native language and in English: "I thank the Creator for giving us this day, I pray for those who have no food, those who have no home, for those who have no family. I pray for all of you who are standing here today, that we are going to make one prayer, that we're going to send one voice, and to thank him for everything that he has given us."[8]

While collective action is the most effective way to address hunger, the individual calling is very powerful. At the Feed the Hungry workshop sponsored by the Archdiocese of Santa Fe in October 2017, Fr. Larry Bernard spoke about a very special person he encountered in the community of Sonsonate, El Salvador. "I met a Franciscan missionary there many years ago who wanted to feed the poor at least a good Christmas dinner. When he succeeded, he was so happy…so delighted in that feast that he determined that no matter how (long) it would take, he would see that the poor and homeless would get a meal every single day."[9]

Dave Miner, a friend with whom I have served on the board of directors of Bread for the World, also offers a beautiful example. A grassroots activist in Indianapolis, Miner started a fifty-meal fast in September 2017 to bring attention to the impact of proposed deep cuts in federal nutrition programs on people in his home state of Indiana. "Every meal I'll miss for the next 16 days represents roughly a million meals in jeopardy for Hoosier children, seniors and veterans if the drastic cuts being debated in Congress now become reality," said Miner. "I have a plan to fast safely. My decision to undertake what I know will be a difficult task is my own choice, while our most vulnerable neighbors could go hungry through no choice of their own. I feel strongly that people of conscience should speak out, in whatever way they feel moved to do so. This is one way I have chosen."[10]

By the grace of God, Miner received the opportunity to offer a much broader witness. In the midst of his fast, the anti-hunger advocate accompanied a delegation from the Indiana Hunger Network to meet with Governor Eric Holcomb. "Dave sat next to the governor during the lunch—in front of an empty plate—while everyone else ate their meal,"[11] said Angie Ruprock-Schafer, a fellow anti-hunger advocate in Indiana.

At times, the call comes in surprising ways. Take the example of Samuel Chu, the lead synagogue organizer for MAZON: A Jewish Response to Hunger. Chu, the son of a Baptist minister in Hong Kong and a graduate of Fuller School of Theology in California, relates how he became the person in charge of advocacy for the largest Jewish anti-

In almost all religious traditions, the connection between our relationship with God and with our neighbor is at the core of our beliefs.

hunger group in the United States. Chu, who once led a primarily Latino Presbyterian congregation in the Koreatown neighborhood in Los Angeles, is certain that his path to MAZON was guided by the Creator. "I have been waiting for you," Chu explained his calling from God during a reflection in June 2017 at the Erev Shabba service at Congregation Albert in Albuquerque.[12] Chu's calling across faith traditions is a great witness on how common values offer a chance for unity, especially in such a basic ministry as providing food to those in need.

For the faith community in New Mexico, the concerns about hunger are front and center. Every year, organizations like Feeding America and the Annie E. Casey Foundation release reports ranking us at the top of the list of states which suffer the most hunger and poverty in the United States.[13] One such report, in 2014,[14] was the impetus for a group of us to create the Interfaith Hunger Coalition. When the findings were made public, we noticed that there was no venue for members of the faith community to come together to discuss common efforts to address hunger. Our initial meeting—which included members of Episcopal, Roman Catholic, Jewish, Mennonite, United Methodist, and Presbyterian congregations—led to the creation of the IHC. Since 2014, our coalition has grown to include members of the Baha'i, Sikh, and Muslim communities, as well as other Christian denominations like the United Church of Christ. Through our joint World Food Day service with NMIPL, we have reached out to members of local Buddhist and Hindu communities.

In discussions, we came to the realization that any efforts to address hunger would need to include secular organizations as well as broader faith-based service and advocacy organizations. Our coalition, which focuses on advocacy and education, has incorporated important organizations like the Lutheran Advocacy Ministry (LAM-New

Mexico), East Central Ministries, Catholic Charities, Lutheran Family Services, the Dialogue Institute Southwest, Roadrunner Food Bank, the Rio Grande Food Project, Feeding Santa Fe, and NMIPL.

By partnering with these organizations, our coalition has sought to create awareness and dialogue about hunger in New Mexico and promote action through advocacy. First Presbyterian Church, Our Lady of the Most Holy Rosary Catholic Community, the Jewish Community Center, Congregation Albert, Presbyterian Women (Presbytery of Santa Fe), Church Women United, and the Albuquerque Baha'i Community have all hosted our Hunger 101 workshops.

Our advocacy committee works closely with LAM-New Mexico to track legislation related to hunger and human needs at the State Legislature in Santa Fe. Our vision is both idealistic and practical: To truly address hunger in New Mexico, we have to take a broad and long-term view. This means working with all the constituencies where hunger is present, including children, seniors, working families, and rural and Native communities.

In February 2018, we took one step in that direction by working with Rep. Sarah Maestas Barnes, a Republican, and Rep. Joanne Ferrary, a Democrat, both members of the Health and Human Services Committee in the State Legislature, to push through a legislative Memorial to create a Hunger Council which will take a broad and long-term approach to addressing hunger in New Mexico. We still have a lot of work ahead of us to make this Legislature-based council a reality. But, as Fr. Larry Bernard says, God wants us to feed the hungry.   •

Love
and Kenosis:
Contemplative Foundations
of Social Justice

By Gigi Ross

ONTEMPLATION AND ACTION begin with love. Contemplation and action end with love. What connects the two and
makes them one is love, and the love linking and undergirding
contemplation and action is the foundation of social justice.

Jesus links contemplation and action in three subtly deeper ways
in the Synoptic Gospels of Matthew, Mark, and Luke, each time com-
bining love of God as stated in the Jewish *Shema*, Deuteronomy 6:5,
and love of neighbor from the Holiness Code of Leviticus 19. I begin
by contemplating the reality of Jesus' words on contemplation—love
of God—and social action—love of neighbor.

JESUS SPEAKS ON CONTEMPLATION AND ACTION

I N MATTHEW 22:34–40, a lawyer tests Jesus by asking which
commandment in the law—there are 613 of them—is the greatest.
Jesus answers, "You shall love the Lord your God with all your
heart, and with all your soul, and with all your mind." This, in essence,
is contemplation: being completely present in love to God and fully
open to God's loving presence within.

It turns out the greatest commandment is not one, but two. Jesus
continues his response, equating loving your neighbor as yourself
with loving God fully and completely. Then he concludes, "On these
two hang all the law and the prophets." The prophets were the voice
of social justice in Jesus' day. For Jesus, trying to obey the commandments or follow the words of the prophets without being rooted and
grounded in love is as impossible as a cloud trying to retain water.
Clouds must release the water they are. God's commandments can
only be carried out in the love that is their source.

In Mark 12:28–34, it's not a lawyer who comes to test Jesus, but
someone who combines legal and theological knowledge. The scribe's
question is slightly different than the lawyer's: "Which commandment
is the first of all?" Unlike the querent in Matthew, he was not simply
seeking a comparison but also wanting to know about beginnings
and sources. "In keeping the commandments, where do we begin?" or
"What is the original commandment?" are other ways he could have
phrased his question, depending on the level of meaning he wished to
draw out. As we'll see in his response to Jesus, this scribe understood
and appreciated nuanced and multivalent expression.

This time, Jesus replies with the entire *Shema*, beginning with
"Hear, O Israel: The Lord is our God, the Lord alone." Oneness is
where Jesus begins his response, and his answer ends with oneness.
God is one, so God's greatest commandment is not only two, but one.
We love God as one, and we are one with our neighbor in love.

The scribe's affirmation—"You are right"—implies he knew the
answer before he asked. He then glosses Jesus' response, confirming
that God is one, and adds there is no other besides God—another
statement with multiple levels of meaning—and that love—loving
God with one's whole being (contemplation), loving others as one-
self (action)—"is much more important than all whole burnt offerings
and sacrifices." This assertion tells us the scribe's query begged for a

qualitative response about origin rather than a quantitative one about rank because, although the laws regarding burnt offerings, sacrifices, and matters related to the temple and temple service far outnumber the other laws Jews of Jesus' day were required to observe, they were of lesser importance. Jesus, acknowledging the scribe's wisdom, concludes, "You are not far from the realm of God."

The test question in Luke 10:25–28 concerns life rather than law. "What must I do to inherit eternal life?" Jesus sometimes used "eternal life" as a synonym for "realm of God," so this question seems related to Jesus' comment that the scribe in Mark was not far from the realm of God. Yet, in reply, Jesus points the lawyer to the law, asking what is written there. The lawyer repeats the words about loving God and neighbor that Jesus used in Matthew and Mark. Jesus, echoing the scribe in Mark, points the lawyer back to life. "You have given the right answer; do this, and you will live." Jesus is not talking about life as an inheritance or future possession but life as something to be lived now. Eternal life is loving God and neighbor now. Living is contemplation and action.

HOW JESUS LIVED CONTEMPLATION AND ACTION

How do we do this, live this love? How did Jesus live it? Through *kenosis*. *Kenosis* is a Greek word, a variant of which is used by Paul when he exhorts the Philippians (2:6–9) to have the same mind as Christ Jesus

> who, though he was in the form of God,
>   did not regard equality with God
>   as something to be exploited,
> but emptied himself,
>   taking the form of a slave,
>   being born in human likeness.
> And being found in human form
>   he humbled himself
>   and became obedient to the point of death—
>   even death on a cross.
> Therefore God also highly exalted him
>   and gave him the name
>   that is above every name.

The word "emptied," a translation of the Greek word *ekenōse*, describes the mind with which Jesus loved God and neighbor, and with which we are called to contemplation and action.

This mindset is not fixed, but a process, a dance that unfolds as follows: a loving recognition of oneness or unity or union with God, letting that recognition go, allowing the sense of separateness to arise, letting it die, allowing the resurrection of the sense of oneness with God, letting it go to repeat the cycle. Readers who practice meditations like Centering Prayer or *Vipassanā* may recognize this cycle.

For Jesus, living contemplation and action begins with oneness, "The Lord our God is one," "though he was in the form of God." This union is ultimately the fruit of loving God. Contemplation is loving God.

Christ did not cling to equality with God, nor use this union to his advantage. He "did not regard equality with God as something to be exploited, but emptied himself." He surrendered his divinity, his power, his privilege, his…until there was no "his," nothing to call his own, nothing to possess, nothing.

Christ became poor and human, unworthy to be born inside a home. He was born with the animals, as if he were a slave, beyond the acknowledgement of those more privileged. In letting go of his low status and humanity, Jesus "became obedient unto death," experiencing complete separation from God when he cried, "My God, my God, why have you forsaken me?" The Latin root of "obedient" is *oboedire*, from *ob*, "in the direction of," and *audire*, "hear." In letting go of divinity and humanity, Jesus continued to listen, his hearing oriented to God's command—and, for Jesus, that command is love.

Jesus completely let go of his human identity and, in doing so, he realized his divinity. "Therefore God also highly exalted him and gave him the name that is above every name." The name that is above every name is God's name. Christ becomes one with God again.

We love God as one, and we are one with our neighbor in love.

This is how Jesus lived contemplation and action. He emptied himself. Love filled the space. He emptied himself. Fear filled the space. He emptied himself. He was hungry. He did not turn stones into bread. He emptied himself.

MY EXPERIENCE OF KENOSIS

D EATH TO RESURRECTION. Divinity to humanity. Independence to interdependence. Having a job, a title, an identity to being unemployed, in poverty, with no accepted or understandable identity. Cycles of *kenosis*.

Kenosis came to me unbidden when I lost my full-time job in 2008 and ran out of money a year later. It came tasting like betrayal, a setup. The job I'd been given was a perfect fit where I lived my call fully, did everything right and well, and then the ground opened up beneath me. Even though I had an intuition I would be asked to empty myself of my position and the identity I'd attached to it, this *kenosis* was not what I wanted. And when the time came to leap into the abyss, my unvoiced "yes" was not wholehearted. The six-year experience of unemployment, poverty, and homelessness that followed stripped me of my willfulness to try to make something happen and filled me with knowing how utterly I am loved by God, by the Universe. This awareness became apparent only when I loved others as I am loved, not just unconditionally but kenotically, with a love that is not mine but which flows through me as I empty myself of expectations, agendas, self-interest, and identity.

That love came in the form of a community to support me on my path and people I met along the way who gave me meals, money, and leads to places to stay. Thanks to this community of God's hands and feet, I did not spend one night on the street nor have a day with nothing to eat. The corollary to loving our neighbor as ourselves is to allow our neighbor to love us. To allow myself to be loved and be dependent on others meant staying empty, and living this empty left me open to be a conduit for God's love in ways I couldn't imagine.

In my last year of living in poverty, I spent two months cat-sitting in a condominium in a suburb just outside of Washington, DC. At the time, the owner needed a cat sitter, and I needed a place to stay. Meeting my need for a place to stay allowed this mother to accompany her son to Johns Hopkins Hospital in Baltimore, where she donated bone marrow for his bone marrow transplant. Having someone stay with her cats saved her added worry about the cats' welfare and the cost of boarding them with someone or a facility, enabling her to devote more energy into being present to her son and to her part in his healing.

The most difficult time of this period, the *kenosis* of *kenosis* for me, was the twenty months I stayed with an activist in her eighties in exchange for helping her continue to live independently in her two-bedroom apartment. She had several chronic health problems and her cognition was noticeably declining. She also regularly participated in protests—against the military's use of drones; Bradley, now Chelsea, Manning's arrest, trial, and sentencing; and Wells Fargo Bank's financing of for-profit prisons, for example. She had set up a trust fund to give away most of her money to charitable nonprofit organizations and her church, keeping just enough for essentials, including rent for an apartment in a building for low-income seniors.

My stay was difficult because the day-to-day details that were my responsibilities mattered less and less to her, and it became more difficult for her to understand the necessity of taking care of them. Secondly, the room where I stayed shared a wall with the apartment next door. The neighbor's television was always on and always loud. I did not sleep well. Poor sleep colored my ability to be present to the woman I was supposed to help.

Six months into my stay, everything came to a head: Unexpected cleaning to be done yet again on my day off. An argument. Angry shouts. Later conversation about what happened. Me not remembering my hurtful words. Once reminded, a vague memory—my wakeup call.

I saw a side of myself that shocked me. I reflected on why I couldn't remember what I knew I had said. I continued my pondering in prayer and spiritual direction. I promised myself never again to take my stress out on her, but to keep it between me and God, who could take my anger without being hurt or thinking ill of me. I only discussed my discomfort with my spiritual director and my closest friends, for broadcasting my irritation too widely would have kept it alive through repeated attention and I wouldn't have had a prayer of emptying myself of my anger. Talking about it too much would have made it more difficult to keep my promise.

I kept my promise and lived there fourteen more months with further opportunities to empty myself. The noise next door continued. I rarely got a good night's sleep or quiet during my morning prayer time. There was no magic wand I could have waved to make myself comfortable. It made as much sense to ask my neighbor to turn down her television as to ask an albatross not to soar. She was hard of hearing and she liked to watch television. I wasn't going to interfere with how she spent her time.

The time came to empty myself of this living situation. The woman with whom I was staying began asking me to do more and more things she used to do. Eventually, it became clear that remaining in the apartment would no longer help her live independently. Fortunately for me, just as I was discerning this, a six-month housesitting opportunity arose.

CONCLUSION

S O H O W D O E S my kenotic life relate to social justice? I'm still living into the answer. I see an obvious connection to social justice when I was helping the activist participating in protests in the name of justice. But the connection goes deeper. I started this essay describing contemplation and social action as aspects of love, and love as the foundation of social justice. This view of love is not original with me. Martin Luther King, Jr., to name one among a host of witnesses, writes in *Stride Toward Freedom* about discovering this same connection through Gandhi's example of *Satyagraha*, which he translated as truth or love force.[1] I've shown how, for Jesus, all of God's commandments come down to love. The major fruit of my time of *kenosis* was a deepening of my capacity to love: to love strangers, to love in discomfort, to love in the unknowing. While I was learning to love kenotically, God's love flowed to others: a social activist in her eighties, a mother with her son who was battling a terminal illness, their cats.

Not only is love the source of contemplation, but contemplation deepens our awareness of love and of God, who is love. For Parker Palmer, an educator and activist, the goal of contemplation is "to help us see through the deceptions of self and world in order to get in touch with what Howard Thurman called 'the genuine' within us and around us."[2] He continues writing that contemplation can be defined in terms of function: "*Contemplation is any way one has of penetrating illusion and touching reality.*"[3] This definition connects with William McNamara's understanding of contemplation as a "long, loving look at the real."[4] The long, loving look at the reality of my anger with the activist was contemplation. I took my anger to God out of love for her and myself, and, in doing so, deepened my love for her and for me. This contemplation emptied me of my anger without removing the stress of that living situation, yet I was empty enough to serve in love.

My *kenosis* of status and home underscored my solidarity with others who live on the margins of cultural norms and expectations. Here is where I find the beginnings of an answer to how my six-year experience relates to justice. I learned that I am marginalized, but not just me. We are all marginalized in some way. This solidarity is the essence of loving our neighbor as ourselves. It leads to the discovery that my neighbor is myself. Interdependence becomes communion. The two commandments become one. Loving my neighbor as myself is loving God with my whole being. God loved is neighbor loved.

My *kenosis* experience was a lived experience of being on the margins. That solidarity with the marginalized was affirmed in my interactions with other homeless people, some of whom commented on my "realness." This sense of communion informs my open, prayerful listening in spiritual direction. It helps shape the projects on which I work. My lived understanding of interdependence infuses my current work at the Center for Action and Contemplation, an organization dedicated to supporting the contemplative dimension of social justice.

May I continue living this love as each leg of *kenosis* unfolds. May we all grow in our love of God and neighbor as we seek to support the reign of justice in our corner of the earth.　　•

"Love and Kenosis: Contemplative Foundations of Social Justice" is an excerpted reprint from Ain't Gonna Let Nobody Turn Me Around: Stories of Contemplation and Justice, *ed. Therese Taylor-Stinson (New York: Church Publishing, 2017), 37–53.*

Christmas Trees, Belonging, and Baptism

By Gideon Tsang

A tree gives glory to God by being a tree. For in being what God means it to be it is obeying Him. It "consents," so to speak, to His creative love.

—Thomas Merton

I F A TREE decorates itself in the forest to fit in with other trees, does it ever truly belong?

Canada has great trees—Christmas trees, to be specific. In the late 1960s, my parents emigrated from Hong Kong to the land of hockey, beavers, and excessive apologies. Being so close to the north pole, Christmas trees looked like a scene out of the movie, *A Christmas Story*. Picture a snow-covered tree, decorated with shiny ornaments, gold garlands, and perfectly wrapped gifts, neatly tucked in to anchor its legs. Now throw in a Chinese family and add thick wool Christmas sweaters.

Despite this backdrop, it took me forty years and a move to Austin, Texas to learn a valuable lesson from a Christmas tree.

Highway 360 is an iconic road among the hills in Austin. It is lined with archetypally Christmas-shaped juniper trees. Most of the year, these trees are overshadowed by the whitewashed limestone walls that hover over the canyon. Decorating these juniper trees for Christmas has become a recent, and growing, tradition.

Inevitably, the Austin Christmas season announces itself when the weather drops below ninety degrees. You can hear the shouts from open windows: "Break out the Christmas sweaters!" Random families load their car with decorations in a chosen theme, descend upon an innocent juniper tree, and dress it up like Liza Minelli getting ready for a night out with Baryshnikov.

These poor trees have been dressed up with Pac-man, Hello Kitty, Bumble Bees, Teddy Bears, and Barbie Dolls. While these Christmas trees live past the post-Christmas cleanup, they endure being decorated with everything from glittering paper plates to pink tulle. They drip with tinsel, ribbons, and self-destructing handmade gifts that sometimes blow across the highway, littering the landscape.

Unfortunately, every season, the enthusiastic decorating has not been met with the same enthusiasm when it comes to cleaning up the décor. In the last few years, a public service announcement has begun to appear on the local news channels: "If you've decorated a tree on 360, you are responsible for cleaning up your decorations!"

I have no experience as a Christmas tree—pine or juniper—but I imagine there is a sense of relief as the decorations are removed. "Finally! You silly humans. Take these ridiculous ornaments off!" I doubt that any of the trees get sent into an existential crisis: "Before the Bumble Bees, I had no sense of who I am as a tree. The black and yellow paper plates really grounded my sense of self. Now that they're gone, in my nakedness, *who am I!*?" The juniper tree is a tree, with or without the decorations.

I wish Thomas Merton was still around to read his words through a megaphone while folks cleaned off their hand-picked trees:

The pale flowers of the dogwood outside this window are saints. The little yellow flowers that nobody notices on the edge of that road are saints looking up into the face of God.... The great, gashed, half-naked mountain is another of God's saints. There is no other like him. He is alone in his own character; nothing else in the world ever did or ever will imitate God in quite the same way. That is his sanctity.... For me to be a saint means to be myself.[1]

Trees have so much to teach me about sainthood.

I REMEMBER WHEN I started decorating myself like a Christmas tree. It was the early 1990s and my Cantonese parents now had three children. I was the middle child, sandwiched between two sisters. We moved to a suburb outside of Toronto in the middle of my freshman year. It was my seventh move in fourteen years of life.

I remember that move cementing the suspicion I've had since puberty: I do not belong anywhere in this world. I showed up on my first day without a school-sanctioned uniform. I walked through a sea of grey pants and white polos in my bright yellow sweatshirt. I felt like Moses parting a sea of Canadian teenagers, all turning their heads to look at the new, weird kid. As I passed, groups of cliques went back to their giggling and gossiping, accompanied by the sound of metal lockers closing. That was it—I didn't belong. I was an Asian kid in a predominately white high school—I didn't belong. I was a short kid who loved to play basketball—I didn't belong. I was a protestant kid in a Catholic high school—I didn't belong. I was a Chinese kid who wasn't good at math(!)—I didn't belong.

After several painful weeks, I finally made one friend—Mark. One day during lunch, he looked across his plate of French fries covered in gravy. As he shook a mound of pepper onto his swamp of potatoes, Mark invited me to a party at his house that night. I looked behind me, unsure that he was talking to me. "You want *me* to come to *your* party?" Knowing all the cool kids would be there, I said yes.

I ran home that afternoon, bursting through the front door, proclaiming my life-changing news. "Who has two thumbs and got invited to a party? This guy!" I announced. My fundamentalist immigrant parents were wary of all things in the world. I could tell by their silence and lack of eye contact that this announcement

If we are unable to accept the differences within ourselves, how are we able to truly accept the differences in others?

scared them. Who knew how much corruption Canadian kids could brainwash into their son during one drunken freshman party? They said, "Of course not!" However, this was my only chance. I would not let my sliver of social hope die. "I'm going!" I replied. After hours of protest and personal activism, my parents relented, setting a strict curfew of 10 pm.

I remember walking down the stairs to the basement of Mark's house. The music of Portishead was playing in the background. Everyone was dressed like a British skinhead from the 1960s—Doc Martens, bomber jackets, and Fred Perry shirts everywhere. A massive dude in the corner had an unlit cigarette tucked over his ear. I remember thinking, "How can anyone in high school look so cool?" (Yes, in hindsight, it was weird that a Chinese immigrant kid was suddenly drawn to neo-Nazi fashion.)

The first two hours of the party were an exercise in post-pubescent awkwardness. A basement full of teenagers sat around, staring at their feet, while people took turns playing a new magic game box called Nintendo. Finally, someone pulled the Nintendo plug, turned up the music, and the party started bumping. I looked at my watch—9:45 pm. I needed to be home in fifteen minutes. I had a decision to make. I could stay at the party and finally make some friends or go home and slumber in my social abyss. I stayed until midnight.

Two strangers in a Volkswagen Cabriolet dropped me off in front of my house. The car drove off before I could awkwardly say good night with a high five. I walked up my driveway, onto the two front steps. The lights were off. This was not a good sign. I opened the porch door, fumbled in the dark, and turned the key to unlock the door. It did not budge. The door was dead-bolted from the inside. I knocked quietly, hoping to awaken my sisters without my parents noticing. It finally sunk in. I was locked out of the house. This was the nail in the coffin. I didn't even belong in my own home.

Not knowing what to do, I sat on the front lawn, staring into the darkness. After several minutes, I got up and wandered the neighborhood alone for the next eight hours. As I walked up and down the silent suburban streets, walled with identical brick houses, groomed lawns, and three-foot trees, I remember loneliness having a palpable weight to it. I can still feel it today. It dawned on me that night: If I don't get my act together, get myself some better decorations, this is what the rest of my life is going to be like. That night set the trajectory for the next thirty years of my life. For the next three decades, it was Project Decoration. How can I get a better personality, hipper clothes, impressive degrees, better-looking friends, interesting stories?

The last thirty years of decoration accumulation have been exhausting.

I F WE NEED to decorate ourselves to fit in with others in community, do we ever truly belong?

I've recently wondered if the meaning of Christian baptism is an invitation for us to reconsider our decorations. The early church baptized its members naked for the first few hundred years, Cyril of Jerusalem (313–386) baptized individuals with these words: "Marvelous! You were naked in the sight of all and not ashamed. Truly you bore the image of the first-formed Adam, who was naked in the garden and not ashamed."[2] Around 400 AD, the Archbishop of Constantinople said, "In this you may know how He enriches your nakedness with His grace."[3] It seemed like nakedness was one of the main points of baptism. Imagine Jesus in his naked form—yes, we're uncomfortable with Jesus' humanity—like an unaccomplished youth, watching as the heavens open to tell him of his Father's affection for him: "This is my Son, the Beloved, with whom I am well pleased" (Matthew 3:17, NRSV).

Baptism reminds us that our worthiness isn't based on our decorations. It has nothing to do with the way we look or don't look, what we can or can't do, our successes or failures, even our talents or inabilities. We are reminded that we are known and loved in our diverse quirks and eccentricities.

If we are unable to accept the differences within ourselves, how are we able to truly accept the differences in others? What if the real challenge of diversity comes in being able to receive love in the parts of ourselves that are embarrassingly different? What if diversity helps us with the most difficult truth about ourselves—that we are actually loved? Can we trust that God loves the strangest parts of us *and* of everyone we ever meet?

May our journey into diversity begin in the naked waters of our baptism. •

My Challenging Journey from Diversity to Unity

By Polly Baca

AS I ENTER my twilight years, I now know that the greatest gift God ever bestowed upon me was the gift of being born a female child to a poor Mexican American family in a bigoted community. This also produced the greatest pain I experienced during my childhood. It was the pain rooted in that experience of bigotry which instilled in my soul a passion to change the way people treated Mexican Americans and, later, the way people treated one another—especially the least among us.

As a child in Greeley, Colorado, I had my own personal relationship with God. When little boys were throwing snowballs at me and calling me a dirty Mexican or little girls taunted me until I cried, I would often ask God why I was born a Mexican American. I believed that was the reason I was rejected by others. It hurt to see signs in stores that read, "No Mexicans or Dogs Allowed."

Then, one afternoon when I was in junior high and walking the mile home from school by myself, I had an overpowering feeling of love for God's earth. I noticed how beautiful the grass and trees were and wondered how anyone could be sad in such a beautiful world. God was my special friend and I enjoyed our constant conversation. I felt that God had a special purpose for me—although I had no idea what that would be.

Now that I have lived more than three quarters of a century, I believe that God has a special purpose for each one of us. We must each discover our own unique mission in life, which I believe is embedded in our True Self, as defined by Fr. Thomas Keating, Fr. Richard Rohr, and other spiritual mystics. For me, it has been through contemplative prayer that I have finally begun to rest with who I am, rather than feeling the burden of having to "show them."

As a young woman in high school and college, I was determined to "show them" by excelling in school. I had not yet developed enough spiritually to understand that the challenges we face can teach us lessons we need for spiritual growth. It's not the challenges that determine our spiritual journey, but rather how we respond to those challenges. My response, at that time, was to get a college education so I could pursue what I believed was my purpose in life: *to transform how Mexican Americans were viewed and improve how we were treated.*

I went to college (1958–1962) on a campus where men outnumbered women seven to one. Out of a thousand graduates, only seven of us were Latinos. The African Americans on campus were mostly football players. I don't recall ever meeting any Asian or Native American students.

It was a time when women, especially Mexican American women, were not expected to go to college, but my parents were determined that their three daughters would get a college education, even though neither of my parents had completed high school. Some of their friends criticized them for being "uppity." They asked, "Why do you want to waste money by sending those girls to college? You know they are just going to get married." Fortunately, my parents ignored the criticism. My mother wanted us to be teachers, a respectable career for women.

We are each a unique creation, expected to love one another across our differences.

My journey changed while I was at college. Initially, I majored in physics, determined to make my mark in the sciences. However, after much soul-searching, I decided that I could have a greater impact by changing my major to political science, where I could learn how to influence public policies that impacted my community. I got very involved in politics and won an internship to work for the state Democratic Party during the 1960 presidential campaign. Much to my amazement, I was able to meet the entire John F. Kennedy clan and their entourage.

When I started college, I didn't know that there was such a thing as daily Mass. Catholic schools in Greeley didn't allow Mexican Americans to enroll. We only received catechism classes, once a week, before we made our sacraments. Many Mexican Americans left the church during that time, but my father said, "You don't leave your faith because of a few bad priests or bishops." My father's unique way of critiquing issues helped form my own independent thinking.

I joined the Newman Club and learned about daily Mass, which was a great solace as I contemplated the purpose of my life. I understood that, as a Mexican American woman, I had been given opportunities to go to college that few women and even fewer Mexican Americans were given. I began to appreciate the fact that many non-Mexican Americans had also encountered challenges. For three of my college years, I lived in a house for low-income women sponsored by the American Association of University Women. Many of my Anglo roommates were low-income women who struggled to make ends meet, just like me.

One evening, at a Miraculous Medal Novena, I had an overpowering feeling of oneness with everyone in the church, regardless of their ethnic or racial heritage. An intense love energy flowed in and through every fiber of my body. That powerful experience led me to inquire whether I should enter a convent and become a nun. Fortunately, our Newman Club pastor suggested that I talk to the nuns at our local Catholic church. He wasn't convinced that I had a vocation as a nun because I was such an activist on campus. After my visit, I decided not to enter the convent.

Although I graduated with honors from Colorado State University, I was not able to get a teaching job. By the time I applied, the quota for hiring Mexican Americans as teachers in the Denver Public Schools had been filled. It seemed that I was destined to do something else.

What I've discovered is that the challenges we encounter are often road maps, pointing us in a direction different than the one we might have planned. If we can open ourselves to trusting the Divine and allowing our lives to unfold, it is amazing what can happen.

Because I could not find a job in Colorado, I reconnected with a young man I had met two years earlier, during the presidential campaign. He helped me get a job in Washington, DC as an editorial assistant for a labor union newspaper—an opportunity that even young white male graduates did not receive.

Getting on a plane at twenty-one years of age and travelling to a city where I knew no one except my boss—with whom I had shared only a four-hour interview—was terrifying. I had never been east of Cincinnati, nor had I ever been on a train or plane. The only thing that gave me the courage to get on that plane—filled with white men in suits—was the belief that this job was an answer to my prayers. I had spent many an hour asking God what I was supposed to do after college. I couldn't believe that God didn't have a purpose for me, given all the opportunities I had received.

The job in Washington, DC marked a dramatic change in my life. As my journey evolved, I was blessed to be part of the labor movement, the civil rights movement, and the Chicano movement. Eventually my feelings of rejection turned to pride as I participated

It is in our diversity that we, together, reflect the beauty of God's one divinity.

in the 1963 March on Washington with Martin Luther King, Jr. and, a few years later, worked with Cesar Chavez and Dolores Huerta as the Co-Chair of the DC Huelga Committee. At times, I was mistaken for being African American because there were so few Mexican Americans in DC.

I was beginning to understand and appreciate the struggles of other minorities. Eventually, I was also awakened to the disparity between men and women. I was at a 1969 conference of grassroots community newspapers, sponsored by the Presbyterians, when the women participants decided to caucus. As I listened to the problems they encountered in the workforce, ranging from sexual harassment to inequity in pay to lack of career promotions, I began to expand my concerns to include the challenges women faced in the workforce. I realized that I had not encountered some of the problems about which they spoke because I was fortunate to have obtained a professional position right out of college.

I N LATER YEARS, I had the opportunity to direct a multicultural leadership development program. It was during this time that some of the participants shared their challenges as members of the LGBTQ community and as white men. Initially, it was easy for me to empathize with the painful experiences shared by other minorities and LGBTQ participants. They often described experiences similar to my own. It was much more challenging to appreciate the problems encountered by straight white men. Yet some of their challenges were often as emotional and difficult as my own. During this time, I learned to listen to those who were not like me.

My involvement with the civil rights movement, the labor movement, the Chicano movement, and the feminist movement eventually led to my returning to Colorado and running for the state legislature. I wanted to have a more direct impact on changing public policies that had a detrimental effect on minorities, women, working families, and low-income people. During my twelve years in the state legislature, I came to realize that we need those who work on the outside, challenging elected officials to pursue just policies, as well as those on the inside, voting on those policies. All are important, including those who focus on praying for those in public office to enact just public policies.

After leaving the legislature, while working for the Clinton Administration, I was introduced to Fr. Thomas Keating and the

Center for Contemplative Living. There I learned Centering Prayer. Then my spiritual journey led me to Fr. Tony D'Souza who, during a retreat, helped me realize that my greatest fear was rejection. That helped me understand my workaholic behavior. Dr. Vie Thorgren helped me understand my life's ordeals by encouraging me to write my spiritual autobiography as I studied to become a spiritual director. Finally, Fr. Richard Rohr and the Center for Action and Contemplation helped me integrate contemplative prayer with my lifelong commitment to action. I began to understand that action born out of contemplative prayer was more likely to be in keeping with God's plan and enhancing of my own spiritual growth.

God has an incredible sense of humor. Paradoxically, we are each a unique creation, expected to love one another across our differences. No two people are identical. This seems to be the most difficult challenge to embrace, yet it can yield the most beneficial lessons.

I had to learn that it was not only Mexican Americans that suffered from discrimination and hardship, but also other minorities, women, LGBTQ, the poor, the disabled, and even some straight white men. I had to learn that pain is not limited to any ethnic or racial group, gender, or particular country. Every human being, regardless of where we live or our distinct circumstances, is challenged with discovering our True Self as we travel our own spiritual journey and fulfill our life's mission.

I believe that each of God's creations manifests a unique part of God's love. It is in our diversity that we, together, reflect the beauty of God's one divinity. That beauty is seen daily in the compassion and love demonstrated by strangers who come to the aid of others, like the young Thai boys trapped in a cave, or the victims of fires and floods. God's love is revealed in these dramatic situations as well as in moments of individual kindness and caring in everyday life.

My journey from diversity to unity has been challenging and gratifying. I am thankful to be a small, unique part of this beautiful tapestry of God's love.   •

Evolving
in Diversity:

A Conversation on Simple Relativity
with Garridon Grady

By Shirin McArthur

Shirin McArthur: What are your thoughts on unity and diversity?

Garridon Grady: I believe that diversity is a fundamental truth of existence. It's one of the wonders of experiencing life as a human being, living the blessing of seeing, hearing, smelling, tasting, and feeling, while floating within the infinite, electric swirl of diversity that is offered in every moment.

Along with all the uniqueness that comprises each moment, there are infinite positions in space and time from which that moment can be observed or experienced. If you consider that each person's life experience at any point is a sum total of all the unique moments made of infinite variables, and only experienced by them at their unique position, you can imagine that our respective collections of experiences are all diverse, unique, and different than anyone else's.

If you take that a step further and apply that line of thinking to the person more like you than anyone else—yourself at any other moment in your life—even then you have a different set of experiences, comprising the perspective in those moments. So, there is even diversity in the set of experiences we ourselves are experiencing and from which we are making decisions, one day, week, and year to the next. I call that out not only to drive home the point that difference and diversity are so persistent in existence that they permeate all internal and external lines, but also to note that accepting and embracing of difference even helps us accept ourselves, and all the decisions and mistakes that we have made.

Diversity is built into the system of existence. In that sense, we are all the same, in that we are carrying a unique load of experiences on our simultaneously parallel, converging, and diverging journeys. If we wish to connect with each other, the earth, the universe, and ourselves, we need to acknowledge, accept, and then embrace that *it is all diversity*. To focus on and let any difference—among the infinite others that exist—create separation between ourselves and another prevents us from achieving true connection to it all. Any connection we make to anything or anyone is inherently an embrace of diversity, and unity is essentially a more universal and unilaterally applied embrace.

Shirin: You have a passion for relativity, which suggests that the laws of physics apply to an object relative to its context and to the viewpoint of the observer. What does relativity teach you about the "other"?

Garridon: Well, for one thing, truth is relative. Simple relativity is a thought exercise I use to let go of some things that I'm really convinced are true—which may absolutely be true, given my perspective—but that doesn't mean that there isn't truth from another perspective on the same object. So, there can be truths from different positions. They can be contradictory but not mutually exclusive. It's relative to the infinite variables that create where I'm sitting and observing something, versus someone one step away, looking at the same thing.

Shirin: So, if truth is relative, how do you address the concept of living with unity?

Garridon: Unity, to me, is ultimately relative, but also a foundational truth of our existence. I can look at humanity from a macroscopic lens and observe our solar system swirling in synchrony with everything else in the universe. No wars are evident, no socioeconomic, racial, or other lines exist. We are absolutely unified in our swirling about the void of space. If I zoom in all the way to earth and far enough to see people in a city on a busy street, I see multitudes moving about in what can appear to be a synchronized, unified dance. We are still unified. Even though any one of those people may hate another, the truth of our unity still exists. We do not collide on foot or in vehicles (mostly!) and are unified in our motion and objective to get where we are going.

So, what does this mean to me? We cannot deny our diversity, unless we choose to pick out a difference and give it arbitrary reverence. We also cannot deny our unity, unless we choose to let some difference or set of differences detach us from the truth of our unity. If we do either, we are creating the state contrary to the true nature of existence, where all is diverse and unified.

The more we strive to live in awareness and alignment to these and other fundamental truths, the more in touch we are with the nature of existence, and with ourselves. I strive for this and I use my relativity thought exercises to evaluate situations, feelings, and circumstances so that I can keep everything in perspective.

Part of that train of thought is what led me to look for more outside of my understanding of Christianity. I started to think that things which were presented as absolute truth were really limiting. When I put them through that test, they just didn't reconcile. I was looking for truths that were broader, more inclusive—foundational truths that, even from many different positions of observation, still reconcile. Those are the ones that I'm really drawn to and focus on.

Shirin: What are some of those? What's withstood the process?

Garridon: As a business graduate student, I'm big into data, analytics, and statistics. The fact that we're even alive, that we even exist,

Diversity is built into the system of existence.

is incalculably improbable. I feel that the universe is good, or positive, tailor-made for us to exist in this moment. Look at it from a science, astrophysics, and mathematical standpoint: The odds are still astronomically weighted against us, that we would exist in this moment. So, that we are taken care of, is one of the foundational truths. This is amazing, and literally a miracle, that we have water floating around in the air that comes down and nourishes us. That is probably the most fundamental one. No matter what the situation is, I can always default to gratitude because I'm existing right now.

Shirin: Do we have any duty or requirement, being human beings, to attempt to move into someone else's perspective?

Garridon: I think so—either intentionally, using that as a mechanism to be more inclusive or connected, or because, through our individual evolution, we end up being more inclusive and connected and therefore able to consider and value other perspectives. It's kind of a "chicken or the egg" conundrum; either one creates the other or the one is a result of the other. I think it's part of evolving as a person. We let go of some of our more rigid judgments or frames of reference that exist in the kind of manmade layer of things, the facade in which we all live.

We only need very basic things in life. Really high on that list, after water, shelter, food, is connection with other humans. How we live is really just us carrying forward some inherited practices as far as society or community. It's all focused on possession—things that, in the end, aren't really doing anything more for us than a spear, a fire, and a tent. As we focus less on that manmade layer and really look at those things that are core to our existence in happiness—which is connection and implied in that is acceptance—there's really no chance that someone's not going to be different from us in some way. So, it's part of evolving toward a more real and sincere existence. We couldn't move down those paths and have deeper connections with external beings that are different without understanding and accepting the differences.

It's a really useful exercise. If I see someone asking for money on the side of the road and they're young and look healthy, I start to apply judgments automatically. In times like these, I put up a filter. "Okay, there's an infinite number of moments that led up to this moment in their life. You're only seeing this one and you have no idea about any of the others." Once I have that thought, it feels silly to apply any judgment.

Shirin: How hopeful are you about our ability to connect, to shift that perspective?

Garridon: I am very hopeful and optimistic and, at the same time, very cynical. I have hope for humanity overall, because I feel like the goodness of existence can't be ignored, especially with globalization, with technology helping people everywhere to connect. Even though we grew up having all our differences magnified, now that we're all able to connect, we start to feel that things are a lot more similar than they are different. So, I hope, in the sense that, over generations, there will be significant improvement.

I don't have a whole lot of hope that there's going to be a massive movement or revolutionary paradigm shift. That's the scale in which it would have to happen to make a difference in our generation, because the systems are so ingrained in our everyday life. There's not a single puppet master. There's not a demon that's doing this or a group of evil people that are controlling this structure. We're all fueling it. Because of that, it's hard to shut it down. There is no single source where we can go to correct the whole system of systems.

That's the cynical part. It's almost impossible to change quickly. But the optimistic part of me says that we are all good, the universe is good, existence is good, and I feel like we're seeing that more.

Shirin: Can you give me an example of where you are seeing it?

Garridon: In my early twenties, when I started looking outside of Christianity for the resonance, it really felt like a solo journey. I felt like I was walking in a shopping mall with all these different stores. There's Buddhism and Catholicism and all these different practices, and I could go in and kind of window-shop and dabble. But it just felt all very separated. I felt like I was walking in the mall by myself, and no one else was looking for the same stuff.

Over time, by way of technology, I started to see that there are a lot more people with that similar kind of yearning, another kind of seeking. That drive is really fueled by that need for connection, looking to connect to some truth and community of people that are on the same journey or are looking for something more real.

When I first heard some of Richard Rohr's stuff, it was like words being put to a lot of the inner dialogue that I'd been going through for that decade—and very concisely and digestibly. That's part of what's giving me hope. I was really reinvigorated by Richard, then by exposure to some of the other teachers in that realm, then by seeing

We cannot
deny our unity, unless
we choose to let differences
detach us from the truth
of our unity.

young people really energized and showing initiative in putting things together.

In general, I see a lot of hope in younger people. From a sense of being able to initiate things, being able to reach out and engage with people, being able to start businesses and organizations, I feel that empowerment is shifting down the age scale a little bit because of accessibility to technology.

Shirin: Where do you want to fit yourself into the hope trajectory?

Garridon: I want to be an enabler. Before I got hired at the CAC, I was doing small business consulting and my wife was doing bookkeeping. That's still something I'm going to do: Empower small businesses, especially startups, with some very sound business principles and in an accessible way. I have plans that leverage technologies that exist in cloud computing. Help them reclaim some of their time, gain some financial freedom, and take one step back from the mechanisms of the machine and hopefully have some time to be present and aware and maybe start down that path of their own evolution. If they're not constantly occupied by having to pay the bills and keep the business open, maybe their life develops elsewhere. Maybe they will spend more time with all the other stuff that really matters.

Shirin: Evolution is a very important term for you.

Garridon: That was actually the most prominent thing that I learned from watching my father. He raised three of us by himself. Over time, I got to see him evolve as a person. He really inspired me in my young life to change how I viewed what I was doing. I always felt that I was a good person. But, in certain periods of my life, there were a lot of negative things happening. I was only focusing on, "Well, but I *am* a good person, so this can't be my fault. I can't be contributing to the cycles of stuff going on in my life." It had me stuck in a victim's perspective.

Then I was inspired by the evolution I saw in my father. It challenged me to think about what I was doing and what role I was playing. Maybe being confident that I'm a good person doesn't also mean that I don't have any work to do. Just because I'm fundamentally sound, as far as my values or intent goes, doesn't mean that's actually the role I'm playing in the world. Maybe what I'm getting back from the world is largely influenced by what I'm doing and how I'm engaging with it. That dialogue will never end.

I feel like the evolution for me is really representative of my path to engage with the world in a way that's as true to my inner self as possible. That's my evolution, my mission: to be as real as possible. •

Unity

There is something dense, united, settled in the depths,
repeating its number, its identical sign.
How it is noted that stones have touched time,
in their refined matter there is an odor of age,
of water brought by the sea, from salt and sleep.

I'm encircled by a single thing, a single movement:
a mineral weight, a honeyed light
cling to the sound of the word "noche":
the tint of wheat, of ivory, of tears,
things of leather, of wood, of wool,
archaic, faded, uniform,
collect around me like walls.

I work quietly, wheeling over myself,
a crow over death, a crow in mourning.
I mediate, isolated in the spread of seasons,
centric, encircled by a silent geometry:
a partial temperature drifts down from the sky,
a distant empire of confused unities
reunites encircling me.

—Pablo Neruda[1]

Beyond Religion:
Insights from LGBTQ Spirituality

By Michelle A. Scheidt

INCREASING NUMBERS of Americans see themselves as spiritual yet choose not to affiliate with a religious tradition. While this shift has become the dominant religious trend of our time, we know little about what it really means to have a spiritual life that is not connected with religious belonging or religious practice. Simultaneously, an equally dramatic social shift has increased awareness and acceptance of people who identify as LGBTQ, a community previously marginalized in the dominant culture. Openly queer people are now visible participants in most facets of public life, including religion and spirituality. These trends—decreased participation in formal religion and increased presence of openly queer people—invite a new understanding of and approach to spirituality. What is spirituality? How do contemporary spiritual seekers engage with questions of meaning, belief, morality, the transcendent, and community outside the traditional structures of religion? This article examines the current religious landscape and ways in which LGBTQ people who are not affiliated with religion experience spirituality. New language and frameworks explore the understanding and experience of spirituality for contemporary spiritual seekers.

A CHANGING RELIGIOUS LANDSCAPE

NUMEROUS STUDIES DOCUMENT a decline in religious belief, practice, and affiliation in contemporary society. Belief in God, prayer, and participation in religious services have decreased, with an even steeper reduction in the percentage of people who are members of a religious tradition. Presently, more than one-fifth of Americans and more than one-third of adults under age thirty do not belong to a religious tradition.[1]

Religious affiliation is even less prevalent among Americans who identify as queer, with higher rates of nonaffiliation and lower rates of Christian affiliation. Data from the Pew Research Center[2] indicate that 41 percent of gay, lesbian, and bisexual people claim no religious affiliation, compared with 22 percent among the straight population. While 72 percent of straight Americans identify as Christian, only 48 percent of gay, lesbian, and bisexual Americans identify as Christian.

As religious affiliation in America has gone down, thousands of churches close every year and less than 20 percent of Americans attend religious services regularly.[3] According to Diana Butler Bass and other religion scholars, the trend is clear: "Traditional forms of faith are being replaced by a plethora of new spiritual, ethical, and nonreligious choices. If it is not the end of religion, it certainly seems to be the end of what was conventionally understood to be American religion."[4]

NEW VOCABULARY

THE GROWING POPULATION of unaffiliated spiritual seekers is religiously and spiritually complex, which has spawned various new terms to describe people who choose not to identify with a religious tradition. Within religion, people readily identify themselves by the name of their tradition, but no common language exists for those outside the traditions. Descriptors popularly used include unaffiliated, nonreligious, secular, none (referring to the option of "no religion"), and spiritual-but-not-religious (SBNR). The acronym SBNR is a fairly new term that begins to fill a gap in the vocabulary. The abbreviation SBNR can be used as both a noun and an adjective, serving as an identifier for individuals and a movement in contemporary Western cultures. SBNR experience is characterized by deep interest in pursuit of spirituality without identifying with a specific religion or religious tradition.

Language has similar complexity among queer people, with a diverse community employing a broad range of self-identifying terminology. Over the past fifty years, language has evolved from "homosexual" and "homophile" to "gay" and "LGBT" as general descriptors to a current panoply of self-identifiers that includes dozens of sexual orientation and gender identity terms. Terms currently in use include lesbian, gay, bisexual, transgender, queer, questioning, intersex, asexual, aromantic, polysexual, pansexual, agender, bigender, trigender, pangender, polygender, nonbinary, genderqueer, ceterogender, demigender, gender neutral, genderfluid, intergender, graygender, genderless, third gender, two-spirit, androphile, gynephile, androgyne, transsexual, pomosexual, and more, with new terms emerging regularly.[5] Queer people may identify with one or more of these identities simultaneously and may also use additional identity markers specific to queer subcultures, such as cross-dresser, drag queen, drag king, leatherman, bulldyke, bear, stone, transman, transwoman, boi, grrl, butch, femme, switch, and various other terms individuals choose for naming their gender and sexual identity.

This rich complexity reflects self-expression and social construction of identity and is not easily captured in a single term. The once-familiar acronym LGBT has thus expanded to become LGBTQ, LGBTQI, LGBTQIA, LGBTQQIIAA, and other proliferations in an attempt to be inclusive. Using "LGBTQ" here is intended as an inclusive term to comprise all minority sexual orientations and gender identities that are not heterosexual and/or not within the gender binary.

The term "queer" may also be used interchangeably with "LGBTQ." "Queer" is in popular usage today as an umbrella term intended to include all people who see themselves as not heterosexual and/or not cisgender. The word "queer" has likewise undergone an evolution in recent decades; once a pejorative used to ridicule, the term has been reclaimed in both popular usage as well as in academic discourse.

The words spiritual/spirituality and religious/religion are also important to this discussion, and may be defined as follows:

> **Spirituality** refers to the inner experience of the fullness of life, a reality greater than the individual self and the physical world, an aspect of human experience through which people seek meaning and transcendence; the spiritual dimension is not limited by religion or dogma and includes relationships with oneself, others in family and society, nature, and the absolute/sacred.[6]

> **Religious** describes those individuals who self-identify as part of organized religion or a specific religious tradition; identifying as religious may include aspects of one's identity, beliefs, practices, ethnic heritage, and group membership among many other qualities.

A FRAMEWORK FOR SPIRITUAL EXPERIENCE

THE COMPLEXITIES OF queer SBNR experience were explored in 2016–2017 through a small research project conducted in Kalamazoo, Michigan. The study included a series of focus groups and interviews with thirteen participants who self-identified as both queer and SBNR. The research revealed a number of common elements in participants' experiences, which led to development of a model of spiritual experience. The model offers a framework to describe spirituality, including two aspects—the inner and the inter-active—which describe the experience of spirituality in everyday life. The initial parameters of the framework appear in Diagram 1.

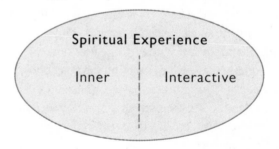

Diagram 1: Framework for Spiritual Experience

The inner and the interactive are two key parts of the spiritual life. The first includes the inner work of seeking personal growth, self-development, maturity, happiness, and wholeness; engaging in individual spiritual practices such as meditation or spending time in nature; intellectual learning; personal ethical choices; and experiencing a sense of oneness with something larger than the self. The interactive includes aspects exterior to the self, such as relationships with others, group spiritual practices, worship, being held accountable, engaging in social action, feeling a sense of connection with the universe, and relational behaviors that take one beyond the self.

The framework further includes nine domains of spiritual experience (see the list in the center of Diagram 2), each of which has inner and interactive aspects. The research participants were asked to articulate their understanding of spirituality, what they think spirituality is; they identified these domains as the ways they live out their spirituality in daily life.

Diagram 2: Framework for Spiritual Experience, with Domains

Two of these domains—transcendence and coming out—are further explored here to help readers understand SBNR spiritual experience from a queer perspective. While these ideas are grounded in the particular experience of the participants in the study, they also offer broader insights about contemporary spirituality and how people describe everyday spiritual experience.

T HE CONCEPT OF God, the divine, or a higher power is not
included in the model, which was a surprising research finding.
When research participants were asked whether and how their
spirituality includes beliefs about a higher power/absolute/some-
thing more than themselves, each group discussed the concept of a
higher power and generally agreed that there is "something more" to
their spiritual experience. The world is more than physical, but what
that "more" is seemed relatively unimportant to define, intangible, and
beyond rational description. The research participants did not want
to limit that "more" they experienced to traditional theistic language.
One participant explained, "Being spiritual to me is just…that sense
of a higher power on some level, whether it's your God or your Jesus
or whatever it is. It's just that…there's a reason, there's a purpose,
there's a lesson, there's always something that you need to give back."

While research participants did not want to eliminate the idea
of a higher power, most seemed to feel that trying to define it is too
limiting. A key idea seemed to be the existence of a larger force, a
transcendence, something ineffable that is beyond the physical world
and holds a deeper meaning. While a traditional theistic conceptual-
ization of the divine was not meaningful to the research participants,
they generally agreed that their experience of the world includes
a non-physical reality. This reality is not personal, not a being, not
authoritarian or controlling, and generally not to be defined. No one
rejected the idea that some type of higher force exists, but the research
participants were more interested in ascribing that realm to mystery
rather than calling it God or having a need to further identify that
ineffable something more; describing it would take away from the
awe and power of the experience of mystery. One participant said, "I
don't believe in a being, but I know I'm not the apex."

"There's a reason, there's a purpose, there's a lesson, there's always something that you need to give back."

CALL TO AUTHENTICITY:
THE EXPERIENCE OF COMING OUT

THE EXPERIENCE OF coming out is a core aspect of the spiritual life for LGBTQ people. When asked about their spirituality, all of the research participants spoke about their experience of coming out as queer. Even though the researchers did not explicitly ask about coming out, participants described coming out as a primary aspect of their spiritual experience, including references to authenticity and being their full selves. All of the participants understood the process of coming out as a key spiritual experience in their lives, describing the need to seek inner coherence, live with integrity, and be authentic to their true self in relating to others. Coming out includes both inner and interactive dimensions as the LGBTQ person comes to understand their identity, accept themselves, and be open about who they are.

Several participants shared painful narratives about having been deeply wounded, emotionally and spiritually, by the experience of concealing their true identities and feeling that they had to hide in order to function in hetero-normative society. This hiding—from themselves, from loved ones, from the larger world—included experiences of shame, identity confusion, feeling judged, feeling different or other, and having a negative self-image. One transgender woman articulated her experience of this inner conflict when she was struggling with her gender transition: "It kept me up at night because I felt like I was not being honest. And I felt like I wasn't being my true self. So my transition—my life radically changed. My husband can tell you, when I came out it was like one day to the next; it was like, the next day, a completely different person."

Coming out is clearly both inner and interactive, as the queer person learns to be themselves and to engage with the people around them, from loved ones to acquaintances to strangers. By coming out, the participants risked rejection and severing of relationships with parents, family, friends, co-workers, religious communities, employers, and broader society. By not coming out, they risked further emotional and spiritual trauma caused by hiding, as one person explained: "The lack of authenticity really hurt me…. I'm telling other people to be strong and be brave and telling other people to be honest and trying to teach my son to be honest, and here I am hiding. That was not good for me spiritually.... It was not good for me in my core. I felt myself starting to wither, sort of, as a person."

IMPLICATIONS FOR THE SPIRITUAL LIFE

WHILE THE EXPERIENCES described here may be unique to the spiritual lives of queer people who identify as SBNR, their insights provide a deeper understanding of spirituality in general. This model of spiritual experience may be applicable to anyone who identifies as a spiritual seeker, with the integration of inner experience and interactive experience across multiple life domains. Understanding aspects of the queer SBNR spiritual experience offers an opportunity for any spiritual seeker, regardless of sexual orientation or religious affiliation, to live with greater integrity and to connect their inner life and their interactive life. The experience of deepening in authenticity, integration, and connection is a valuable pursuit for anyone seeking spiritual growth. In addition, considering perspectives from a diversity of backgrounds helps to expand thinking and to create openness to new possibilities for what religion and spirituality might be; this exercise in itself can be a spiritual practice leading to profound growth.   •

This article is drawn from Michelle Scheidt's Doctor of Ministry thesis research, completed in 2017 at Chicago Theological Seminary.

Universal Healthcare as a Divine Right:

An Elegant Expression of Unity in Diversity

By David M. Cook

This article is dedicated to all the souls working tirelessly, in the space of health and healthcare, to be the change they wish to see in the world. Two such beautiful souls, Dr. Ophelia Garmon-Brown and Dr. Susan Funk, are alumni of the Center for Action and Contemplation's Living School. Both draw upon a spirit-filled approach to heal the body, mind, and soul. Each continues to work diligently to create universal healthcare.

Kudos to your example, and may we each strive to be as courageous, determined, and loving in the search for unity in diversity and transforming our future.

Truly I tell you, whatever you did for one of the least of these brothers and sisters of mine, you did for me.

—Matthew 25:40, NIV

LOVE, PEACE, TRUTH, unity, and diversity were some of the founding principles of Jesus' way of life. He knew that the universe was a web of consciousness founded upon unity and harmony, supported by love. He knew that what happened in the heart was more important than what happened in the head. By living from the heart, he knew one could see the Divine in all things.

Knowing this, we can better understand what Jesus was saying in Matthew 25:40 and become aware of its deeper meaning. This understanding opens us to experience a profound transformation in our own lives, thus affecting the way we show up for others, the planet, and the universe. Within our current economic, political, and cultural complexities, this transformation is truly the first step in finding a solution to the challenges we face in healthcare today.

Despite profound advances in technology, tremendous wealth, religious fervor, and altruistic initiatives, we face a grim reality of healthcare disparities and health inequities in the United States. These inequalities are based on gender, gender identity, race, ethnicity, age, income, and personal resources. These disparities can, and often do, lead to generational poverty, systemic exclusion, ongoing racism, isolation, increased pain and suffering, increased mental illness, reduction in length and quality of life, and lack of joy and freedom, to name but a few.

When I speak of universal healthcare or universal health coverage, I am referring to equal access for all people to excellent healthcare, not substandard care. Universal healthcare is the foundation for eradicating healthcare disparities and health inequities. This care cannot create a financial burden or hardship that results in emotional distress, persistent poverty, exclusion, increased pain, or unintended suffering.

How can we continue to deny individuals healthcare in 2018, no matter the reasoning? How can such disparities and inequities continue to exist in one of the richest countries in the world, a nation that prides itself on equality, progressiveness, and freedom?

"The three most difficult things for a human being are not physical feats or intellectual achievements. They are, first, returning love for hate; second, including the excluded; third, admitting that you were wrong."[1] These are also difficult things for a community, society, and nation.

Many people would argue that the American healthcare system is the best in the world. It is true that our "rescue" or allopathic system of care has led to miraculous cures and the eradication of many diseases. However, this same system has created gross profiteering and wealth-gathering, a "sick-care" model instead of a model promoting health, a brokering of individual health on Wall Street, fee-for-service versus value-based care, exorbitant drug costs, and roughly one trillion dollars in annual waste. Issues such as these have led to exclusion, separation, dualistic thinking, persistent poverty, and systemic racism, and have forced many to make heart-wrenching decisions between their individual health and feeding, clothing, and housing their families.

It is apparent that we have missed Jesus' message and instead are caught up in complex economic, social, and political systems that continue to produce exclusion and create devastating outcomes for those excluded. These excluded are often found on the fringe of mainstream society, represented by the poor, elderly, homeless, refugees, minorities, or a particular ethnic group. Ironically, those on the fringe suffer from a lack of voice, while also being laden with the heaviest burden of disease.

As Christians, contemplatives, and spiritual beings, we must see that Jesus' message in Matthew speaks directly to the divine right of universal health coverage. We can no longer tolerate leaving anyone behind in healing the body, mind, and soul. We must return love for hate, include the excluded, and admit we may have been wrong.

Jesus saw the "least of these" as the excluded, those on the fringe or those on the bottom. He did not consider them as being "less than" anyone else. He saw them as one with himself and not as a cause or

We must see that Jesus' message in Matthew speaks directly to the divine right of universal health coverage.

concept in need of fixing. When we, as individuals and society, have an awareness and understanding of the underlying unity in human diversity, the problem fixes itself. As said by many homeless individuals, the greatest pain and suffering comes not from illness, hunger, or exposure, but from not being seen. Jesus saw them and, in doing so, he laid the foundation for "bottom-up spirituality," which most of us miss en route to power, wealth, and success. Unfortunately, it is all too easy to miss the "bottom" on the path to nirvana, awakening, or spiritual superiority.

Jesus certainly believed in, and practiced, universal healthcare, without relenting to the pressure of those who questioned his practice. An example was the lepers who were excluded by the high priests, Roman officials, and power brokers of the day. As is true now, leaders use their religion or policies to exclude those who do not look like, think like, or act like themselves. Many sages, prophets, and mystics have spoken against this practice of using policy and religion to justify separateness, racism, exclusion, and oppression. Mother Teresa (1910–1997) was one of these holy people who lived bottom-up spirituality in the poorest region of the world and often used Matthew 25:40 to describe her work with the excluded.

BEFORE WE CAN and will change any system, we must first change what is inside of ourselves. Real inner transformation takes us out of fear and into Love—out of the ego and into the heart. The more we live in fear, the stronger the ego becomes and the less capable we are of returning love for hate. The ego is created and fed by our false beliefs. These false beliefs about ourselves, others, and the world create attachments to material things such as money, power, prestige, authority, and even precious healthcare resources. It is by acting from false beliefs that we can justify the unequitable sharing of healthcare resources and justify that, for some, these resources must be earned. Where is God in this thinking, belief, or behavior?

The human body is the sacred vessel for the soul, a soul which is ever seeking union with the Divine and oneness with all creation. When filled by Spirit, our souls grow, expand, and merge with the Divine, with one another, and with all things. Healing occurs only when we bring Spirit and soul into the process with body and mind. Jesus knew this to be true. His message on healing was very simple and did not involve complex structures or systems. He did not exclude or deny care, he did not judge those in need of care, and he did not set up a religion to justify inequality. He simply wanted each of us to be free from suffering and to find the peace that endures the most difficult trauma, illness, or loss.

Before we react to or fight against a broken system, let us take the inward journey to freedom, humility, and love. This is the only journey that will lead us to unity and real solutions. This was and is Jesus' simple, yet profound, message of transformation. We can be instruments of peace if we ourselves have peace within. We can best heal others and the world if we ourselves are healed. With this trans-formation, we will know our connection to all beings, despite human differences. Once we see Divinity in all beings, diversity becomes a contrast that leads away from separation. We are given diversity to see the possibility of unity more completely and the contrast provided by diversity is fertile ground for a soul's growth toward Divinity. This is hard for most of us to grasp, living in a culture of power, competition, winning, and "rugged individualism." If we can really awaken to this truth, we will see and know the unity in all diversity and the need for diversity to see the oneness in all.

What is our responsibility, as a country, as contemplatives, and as spiritual beings, in the cultural and political environment in which we find ourselves? First, as believers in oneness and non-duality, we must not complicate the issue. We cannot judge how we arrived here, but believe history will judge us harshly if we do not take this oppor-tunity to wisely, humbly, and heartfully change the future for the highest good!

It is time for a third way to prevail. There can be no more excuses, no matter how relevant they seem, that prevent us from working together to create equal access to extraordinary, spirit-filled care. We must create a healthcare system that does not discriminate based on differences, but uses the Law of Abundance to build a foundation of diversity, unity, and love. Upon this foundation we can create a system that is reflective of the Divine in each of us and leads to real health for individuals, communities, and our nation.   •

The Vicarious Trauma of Hate

By LaVera Crawley

Small sorrows speak. Great ones are silent.
—Seneca the Younger

O<small>N</small> M<small>AY</small> 16, 2018, my travel companions and I visited the infamous *Haus der Wannsee-Konferenz*, a magnificent villa in the tony suburbs of Berlin near Lake Wannsee. We were a group of American and European scholars (physicians, ethicists, and historians) gathered in Berlin as a sort of think-tank, each of us sharing a curiosity about pre-World War II German medical history and what it could teach us about the global contemporary trend toward legal-izing physician-aid-in-dying. Sponsored by the Center for Medicine after the Holocaust, our focus was the moral drift to which German society had fallen prey during that historical period, shepherded in no small part by its medical societies and German doctors, nurses, and other providers.

These groups were critical players—engineers and implementers of Germany's eugenics crusade for racial hygiene which manifested early on as sophisticated public health propaganda campaigns and later through the promotion of the sterilization and racial laws aimed to protect German purity and honor. These efforts would give way (although clandestinely) to the involuntary euthanasia programs aimed at removing "defective" German citizens—mentally and physically disabled adults and children—who were deemed to be "lives unworthy of living." Horrific in themselves, these precursors to terror were evidence of the slippery slope that would ultimately lead to what they euphemistically referenced as "evacuation" protocols that attempted to exterminate the entire Jewish population of Europe.

Among the members of my group were physicians in the professional trenches of palliative care work, a few being American proponents and practitioners of physician-assisted suicide, along with one or two of their European counterparts who advocated for or had even administered euthanasia. However, most of us were opposed to the practices, although not all for the same reasons. As a physician, ethicist, chaplain, and the only African-American in the group, I wanted to use the study tour as an opportunity to revisit and dive deeper into my previous scholarship on race-based inequities in American healthcare in light of the current Black Lives Matter movement. The full group had only met for the first time just two days prior, and so the drive to Wannsee was still mainly cordial, superficial, get-to-know-you chatter. I enjoyed the conversations, but my attention was also drawn to the natural beauty of the passing scenery as we left behind the urbanity and architectural splendor of Berlin and headed toward its famed forests and residential suburbs near the lake.

En route, our tour guide insisted that we make an impromptu stop before our planned activities for the day—the trip to Wannsee House, followed by an insider's tour of the Sachsenhausen concentration camp. We stepped off our tour bus at Grunewald Train Station, a former freight yard that served as one of three deportation points for Jews who'd been unable to flee Berlin before the forced evacuations began. We headed toward Track 17 to view a memorial that had been erected on the site. There didn't seem to be much to see at first—overgrown vegetation surrounding an abandoned platform, tucked away on the side of the active rail station, upon which had been lain a series of large, cast steel grates. Scattered about were smaller, more personal memorials—a few bouquets of flowers, now dried and withered, and several empty, bright, blue-and-red cans, labeled in Hebrew, with bits of residual wax from candles that had previously burned inside the cans.

There was a solitude and an eeriness I couldn't quite name. We were alone and no one made a sound as we each walked separately, meditatively along the footpath beside the tracks. I soon noticed the inscriptions on the steel grates, each one marked chronologically by the day, month, and year of a particular transport, along with the number of Jews deported and the site of their final destination—names like Riga, Auschwitz, Sachsenhausen, and other ominous places. There were 186 of these cast steel grates, representing over fifty thousand Berlin Jews who were "evacuated" in the years between 1941 and the end of the war.

27.11.1941 | 1035 JUDEN | BERLIN-RIGA. Looking at the inscriptions, I tried to imagine what it must have been like to be made to forcibly stand at that very platform, in the cold, on November 27, 1941, accompanied by 1,034 terrified others, each with the one or two pieces of luggage that could be carried on board by hand and each precariously awaiting deportation to the Jewish ghetto in Latvia (Riga) with no idea of what would happen next.

I was piecing together facts, conjuring pictures in my mind from photographs I'd seen in books, and trying to fathom what it must have been like.

1.3.1943 | 1736 JUDEN | BERLIN-AUSCHWITZ. March 1, 1943. By now, word had spread regarding the fates of those sent to the infamous Polish death camp. Was there any hope of survival among the 1,736 men, women, and children standing there on that day?

5.1.1945 | 20 JUDEN | BERLIN-SACHSENHAUSEN. January 5, 1945. The end of the war loomed, and the Nazi Party knew they had lost. Very few Jews remained in Berlin, yet evacuation transports were still taking place. Surely, the twenty Jews standing on Track 17 knew by now the terrible fate that awaited them.

For me, the Holocaust had previously existed only as abstract history: horrific, yes, but as mere facts and mental constructs of a grim past reality—not my personal reality. Standing there on the platform at Grunewald Station, however—amidst the phantoms of tens of thousands of victims of humanity's inhumanity—the reality of others' experiences reached through time and touched me deeper than my intellect could bear. Something inside me broke on that platform.

A great sorrow had silenced me, as there were no words to capture my emotional anguish. We were all silent during the short ride between Grunewald and Wannsee. As we got closer to the lake, the lush neighborhoods, stunning homes, and idyllic gardens caught my attention again. While the appeal provided some cognitive distancing from the profound despair that had just surfaced on Track 17, the contrast felt dissonant. *Such depravity amidst such beauty.*

Even the elegance of our destination, the *Villa Am Großen Wannsee* 56–58, was completely and utterly disorienting. This grand house marked the denouement of the nefarious slippery slope we had come to study. It was here, on January 20, 1942, that the Wannsee Protocol—the means, methods, and coordinated efforts needed to implement the "final solution to the question of the Jews"—was planned and agreed upon by fifteen high-ranking members of the Nazi party, the SS (Nazi police), and other government bureaucrats. To them, the Jews, along with gays, Romani (gypsies), the disabled and mentally ill, and other non-Aryans, were considered subhuman, some even lower than animals. This was how they justified the blueprint for the atrocities they committed.

> *It happened once and it can happen again.*
> *This is the heart of what we have to say.*
> —Auschwitz survivor Primo Levi

I RONICALLY, ON THE same day we visited Grunewald and Wannsee, another event across the globe was taking place that bore a terrifying resemblance to the history about which we were learning. Back home in the United States, the White House was convening a round-table discussion with state officials, local mayors, and law-enforcement leaders from my home state of California who opposed the state's sanctuary laws. These laws were a compassionate response to the hard line that the Trump administration has taken on immigration and an attempt to comfort families in California who have become terrorized, living in fear of being split apart, deported, or worse. At the meeting and in the presence of the press, Donald Trump spoke

Is this how the average German citizen reacted during the times leading up to and during World War II? Did they just tune it out?

about immigrants as he had during his entire presidential campaign. "You wouldn't believe how bad these people are. These aren't people, these are animals and we're taking them out of the country at a level and at a rate that's never happened before."[1] The rhetorical similarities were frightening and represented what Fr. Richard Rohr has called the "undying recurrence of hatred of the other."[2]

With all my knowledge, training, and life experiences—particularly as a Black woman in her sixties—I thought I was prepared for the intellectual, psychological, and emotional challenges of studying the Holocaust. But standing broken and silenced on the platform in Grunewald suggested otherwise. I returned home traumatized, insidiously at first. I noticed problems sleeping, but assumed it was due to international travel and the extremely busy workload that greeted me on my return. Gradually, other signs began surfacing. I had difficulty concentrating. I became lax in my spiritual practices. My students began pointing out to me that I had become overly critical and impatient; my family experienced me as harried and distant. Inwardly, I felt existentially lost and full of ennui. When I finally recognized that I was emotionally paralyzed and couldn't cry, I knew that something profoundly negative was happening to me.

The worst was the relentlessly overwhelming sense of impotence and guilt. Being bombarded daily by headlines and harrowing images of innocent children being separated from their parents and sent to detention centers was too much for me to take in. I felt small and incapable of making any difference in a problem that seemed well beyond my reach. I just wanted to tune it all out and withdraw—but then I wondered: Is this how the average German citizen reacted during the times leading up to and during World War II? Did they just tune it out? I learned that the Germans have a great word for it: *Totgeschwiegen*, or "deadly silence." This thought convicted my soul.

I was displaying symptoms of what psychotherapists call vicarious trauma—changes in behavior and personality because of empathic engagement with the trauma of others. It's not an uncommon experience for those of us in the helping professions. For me, it resulted from spending nearly two weeks in Germany, visiting psychiatric hospitals where the mentally disabled were experimented on and euthanized, gas chambers where thousands of innocent people died, concentration camps, crematoriums, and memorials, and studying primary-source materials and records that documented the abominable atrocities committed by the German government and its people.

Healing from vicarious trauma is an ongoing work in progress and I imagine it will need to be a lifelong endeavor as I stay committed to doing justice work. The most important first step for my recovery has been to accept what this is: an eye-opening change in worldview and a further invitation to radical servanthood. I have needed to re-commit to practices—contemplative and action-oriented—that support resilience and wholeness; not only for myself, but for the larger community as well. For example, I have reached out to family, to my community of friends and colleagues, and to my therapist for help. My husband and I connected with our local Sanctuary movement and recently joined an immigrants'-rights protest at a nearby detention center. Writing this essay as a means of sharing my story has been cathartic and allowed the tears to flow freely again. Staying grounded in the Holy Spirit and obedient and hopeful in love, my healing has begun.   •

Mother Yemen

To you I bring my empty
beggar's bowl
And to you I bring my bowl
filled with children's tears

I beseech you and ask
Don't let my child starve
to death
Nothing's left of her but
her eyes vacant with life
and a thin layer of skin
covering her brittle bones

I beg you to fill my
beggar's bowl with one
ounce of compassion
I take my bowl door to door
from city to city
from country to country,
but, no one hears me
no one listens

It's too late for my child.

But,
maybe one day
your fortified walls
will crumble
and you will hear the voice

of the mothers and
you will hear the
plea of the children.

Maybe one day,
No mother will see her
child starve in her arms
Or, see her child blown
to pieces before her eyes
or kidnapped by mercenaries of war,
warehoused for organ harvesting
or auctioned off to pimps and pedophiles.

I take my bowl door to door
from city to city
from country to country.

Maybe, just maybe,
One day my beggar's bowl
will be filled with compassion
and my other bowl will be
empty of children's tears.

—Avideh Shashaani[1]

RECOMMENDED READING

Exclusion & Embrace:
*A Theological Exploration of Identity,
Otherness, and Reconciliation*

Miroslov Volf
Abingdon Press, 1996

A Book Review by Lee Staman

Professor Miroslav Volf had just finished a lecture when his mentor, Jürgen Moltmann, posed a question: "But can you embrace a *četník?*" It was 1993 and, for Volf (a Croat), the Serbian *četníks* had been instrumental in what would later be known as the Bosnian Genocide. Up to that point, Volf had been arguing on the need for us to embrace our enemies as God had embraced us in Christ. The question was a personal one and, after some time, Volf answered honestly, "No, I cannot—but as a follower of Christ I think I should be able to."[1]

Exclusion & Embrace is Volf's attempt to formulate a response to our encounter with the other. By exploring the idea of exclusion, in its many forms, and then constructing a robust answer, Volf proposes an innovative and challenging theological answer. For Volf, "It may not be too much to claim that the future of our world will depend on how we deal with identity and difference."[2]

Volf begins his effort by defining exclusion as, "barbarity within civilization, evil among the good, crime against the other right within the walls of the self."[3] He sees three distinct types of exclusion: (1) exclusion by elimination, along with its less-aggressive side, assimilation; (2) exclusion by domination through assigning the other the status of inferior being; and (3) exclusion by abandonment, specifically in how the wealthy of the West relate to the poor.

Exclusion is distinct from oppression in this definition. For Volf, oppression is born of economic and political exploitation and is tied with liberation. The problem begins when both sides can claim oppression or, when the oppressor is defeated, the liberator and oppressor may have to continue living together. In Volf's words, "the categories of oppression and liberation provide combat gear... they are good for fighting, but not for negotiating or celebrating."[4] These categories make true reconciliation difficult and take the ultimate goal—which is love, not freedom—even further out of reach (see Gustavo Gutiérrez, A Theology of Liberation and Jürgen Moltmann, The Trinity and the Kingdom). While liberation has its place, Volf stresses that it must fit into a larger "theology of embrace."

The highlight of Exclusion & Embrace is the exposition of a true embrace. For Volf, "the will to embrace is unconditional and indiscriminate."[5] The first act of what Volf calls "The Drama of Embrace" is the act of opening the arms. His simple description, that "open arms suggest the pain of the other's absence and the joy of the other's anticipated presence,"[6] is as beautiful as it is insightful.

The second act is waiting. This is the tough one. We are vulnerable, but cannot rest on any guarantee that our first act will be reciprocated. "If embrace takes place, it will always be because the other has desired the self just as the self has desired the other."[7] This is where hope and patience are borne out.

The third act, closing the arms, carries with it one of Volf's more interesting notions. "To preserve the alterity of the other in the embrace it is essential to acquire the unusual ability not to understand the other."[8] There can be no presumptions. We must let the unknown be and, more importantly, let the other be.

The fourth act, of opening the arms, brings the drama full circle. "The open arms that in the last act let the other go are the same open arms that in the first act signal a desire for the other's presence.... They are the same arms that in the second act wait for the other to reciprocate, and in the third act encircle the other's body.... Though embrace itself is not terminal, the movement of the self to the other and back has no end."[9]

Volf's potential way forward is as challenging as the question Moltmann posed to him—probably even more so. There are aspects of forgiveness, forgetting, history, and remembering that challenge even Volf in this book. In the end, the choice is simple, but far from easy: "To agree on justice you need to make space in yourself for the perspective of the other, and in order to make space, you need to want to embrace the other. If you insist that others do not belong to you and you to them, that their perspective should not muddle yours, you will have your justice and they will have theirs; your justices will clash and there will be no justice between you."[10]   •

NOTES

Embracing Diversity through the Cosmic Principles

1 Thomas Berry, *The Great Work: Our Way into the Future* (New York: Crown, 1999), 110.

2 Beatrice Bruteau, *The Holy Thursday Revolution* (Maryknoll, NY: Orbis, 2005), 6.

3 Francis, *Laudato Sí* (Washington, DC: United States Conference of Catholic Bishops, 2015), 138.

4 Ibid.

5 Berry, *The Great Work*, 149.

Half-and-Half

1 Naomi Shihab Nye, "Half-and-Half," *19 Varieties of Gazelle: Poems of the Middle East* (New York: HarperCollins, 2005), 96. Used with permission of the poet.

Unity and Diversity in the Land of Nonviolence

1 Mahatma Gandhi, *Young India*, December 4, 1924.

For You and for Me

1 Jonathon Stalls, "For You and for Me." Used with permission of the poet.

The Narratives that Make Us

1 James H. Cone, *The Cross and The Lynching Tree* (New York: Orbis, 2013), 166.

2 Jacqueline J. Lewis, *The Power of Stories: A Guide for Leading Multiracial and Multicultural Congregations* (Nashville: Abingdon, 2008), 62.

3 James Baldwin and Nikki Giovanni, *A Dialogue* (Philadelphia: Lippincott, 1973), 22.

1 Larry Bernard, "God Wants Us to Feed the Hungry," *Bread New Mexico Blog*, October 3, 2017, http://breadnm.blogspot.com/2017/10/god-wants-us-to-feed-hungry.html.

2 "Our Messages from the Interfaith Hunger Coalition via YouTube," *Bread New Mexico Blog*, October 1, 2017, https://breadnm.blogspot.com/2017/10/our-messages-from-interfaith-hunger.html.

3 Ibid.

4 Allen S. Maller, "Rabbi Maller: How Fasting Connects Islam and Judaism," *MuslimVillage.com*, June 22, 2016, https://muslimvillage.com/2016/06/22/119048/rabbi-maller-fasting-connects-islam-judaism/.

5 "Our Messages."

6 David Langness, "Recognizing the Spiritual Benefits of Fasting," *BahaiTeachings.org*, March 4, 2018, http://bahaiteachings.org/recognizing-spiritual-benefits-fasting.

7 "Our Messages."

8 "A Lakota Prayer for the Well-Being of Humanity," *Bread New Mexico Blog*, October 28, 2016, https://breadnm.blogspot.com/2016/10/a-lakota-prayer-for-well-being-of.html.

9 Bernard, "God Wants Us."

10 "When the Governor Invites You to Lunch . . . and You're Fasting," *Bread New Mexico Blog*, September 29, 2017, http://breadnm.blogspot.com/2017/09/when-governor-invites-you-to-lunchand.html.

11 Ibid.

12 "I Have Been Searching for You," *Bread New Mexico Blog*, June 17, 2017, https://breadnm.blogspot.com/2017/06/i-have-been-searching-for-you.html.

13 For example, see Thomas C. Frohlich, "States Where the Most Children Go Hungry," *USA Today*, April 27, 2014, https://www.usatoday.com/story/money/business/2014/04/27/states-where-children-hungry/8151905/.

14 As reported in Rick Nathanson, "NM Tops in Childhood Hunger," *Albuquerque Journal*, April 29, 2014, https://www.abqjournal.com/391263/nm-tops-in-childhood-hunger.html.

Love and Kenosis: Contemplative Foundations of Social Justice

1   See Martin Luther King, Jr., *Stride Toward Freedom* (San Francisco: Harper and Row, 1986), 96–97.

2   Parker J. Palmer, "Contemplative by Catastrophe," *On Being with Krista Tippett* (blog), November 11, 2015, https://onbeing.org/blog/contemplative-by-catastrophe/.

3   Ibid. (emphasis in the original).

4   William McNamara, as quoted by Walter J. Burghardt, "Contemplation: A Long, Loving Look at the Real," *Church*, No. 5 (Winter 1989), 14–17.

Christmas Trees, Belonging, and Baptism

1   Thomas Merton, *New Seeds of Contemplation* (New York: New Directions, 1961), 30.

2   Cyril of Jerusalem, *Works of Saint Cyril of Jerusalem*, trans. Leo P. McCauley and Anthony A. Stephenson (Washington, DC: Catholic University of America Press, 1969), 2:162.

3   Johannes Quasten and Walter J. Burghardt, Jr., eds., *Ancient Christian Writers: The Works of the Fathers in Translation* (Mahwah, NJ: Paulist, 1963), 31:228.

Unity

1   Pablo Neruda, "Unity," in Clayton Eshelman, ed. and trans., *Conductors of the Pit: Artaud, Holan, Césaire, Vallejo, Csoori, Breton, Neruda, Radnoti, Rimbaud, Hierro, Bador, Juhasz, Szocs* (Berkeley: Counterpoint, 2005), 11. Used with permission.

Beyond Religion: Insights from LGBTQ Spirituality

1   Pew Research Center, "'Nones' on the Rise: One-in-Five Adults Have No Religious Affiliation," *The Pew Forum on Religion and Public Life*, October 9, 2012, http://www.pewforum.org/files/2012/10/NonesOnTheRise-full.pdf.

2   Pew research data include only those who identify as gay, lesbian, or bisexual, leaving out transgender people and other sexual orientation and gender minority groups.

3   Steve McSwain, "Why Nobody Wants to Go to Church Anymore," *The Huffington Post*, US Edition, The Blog, updated January 23, 2014, http://www.huffingtonpost.com/steve-mcswain/why-nobody-wants-to-go-to_b_4086016.html.

4 Diana Butler Bass, *Christianity After Religion: The End of Church and the Birth of a New Spiritual Awakening* (New York: HarperCollins, 2012), 14.

5 Marilyn Roxie, "Genderqueer and Non-Binary Identities & Terminology," *Genderqueer and Non-Binary Identities*, updated July 24, 2015, http://genderqueerid.com/gq-terms.

6 Ursula King, *The Search for Spirituality: Our Global Quest for a Spiritual Life* (New York: Bluebridge, 2008), 4–8.

Universal Healthcare as a Divine Right:
An Elegant Expression of Unity in Diversity

1 Anthony De Mello, *Awareness*, ed. J. Francis Stroud (New York: Image Books, 1992), 59.

The Vicarious Trauma of Hate

1 Julie Hirschfeld Davis, "Trump Calls Some Unauthorized Immigrants 'Animals' in Rant," *New York Times*, May 16, 2018, https://www.nytimes.com/2018/05/16/us/politics/trump-undocumented-immigrants-animals.html.

2 Richard Rohr, "Introduction," *Oneing* 6, no. 2 (2018): 13.

Mother Yemen

1 Avideh Shashaani, "Mother Yemen," June 3, 2018, https://www.youtube.com/watch?v=W83wIhCR9No. Used with permission of the poet.

Exclusion & Embrace:
A Theological Exploration of Identity, Otherness, and Reconciliation

1 Miroslav Volf, *Exclusion & Embrace: A Theological Exploration of Identity, Otherness, and Reconciliation* (Nashville: Abingdon, 1996), 9.

2 Ibid., 20.

3 Ibid., 60.

4 Ibid., 103.

5 Ibid., 215.

6 Ibid., 141.

7 Ibid., 143.

8 Ibid., 143.

9 Ibid., 145.

10 Ibid., 220.

Coming Spring 2019!

The Universal Christ, Vol. 7, No. 1

From Richard Rohr's Introduction:

Most of us were given the impression that Christ was Jesus' last name. We were presented with "the historical Jesus" (largely in the synoptic Gospels of Matthew, Mark, and Luke), not fully realizing we had already been presented with *a ubiquitous Christ* in Paul's letters (which preceded all the Gospels) and a rather *archetypal and larger-than-life Christ* in the later Gospel of John and the Book of Revelation.

Christ is our word for the universal principle of truth and the process of growth (death and resurrection), just like *Logos* or *Tao*. Christ is good and even necessary for one coherent history and society. "In him [*sic*] everything in heaven and on earth was created, things visible and invisible" (Colossians 1:16) (although Christ is not a "him" at all, but beyond all gender [Galatians 4:28], which solves many of our useless gender arguments about the Incarnation).

This limited print edition of CAC's literary journal, *Oneing*, will be available April 2019 at https://store.cac.org/.

Center for
Action and
Contemplation

A collision of opposites forms the cross of Christ.
One leads downward preferring the truth of the humble.
The other moves leftward against the grain.
But all are wrapped safely inside a hidden harmony:
One world, God's cosmos, a benevolent universe.